NOËL AND GENTIL

NOËL AND GERTIE

An entertainment devised by

Sheridan Morley

with the words and music of

Noël Coward

OBERON BOOKS
LONDON

First published in this edition in 1997 by Oberon Books Ltd
(incorporating Absolute Classics),
521 Caledonian Road, London N7 9RH.
Tel: 0171 607 3637 / Fax: 0171 607 3629

Copyrights on the musical work: NOËL AND GERTIE

Book of the work – devisor – Sheridan Morley © 1993

POETRY AND PROSE	DATE OF COPYRIGHT
Present Indicative	1937 – Estate of Noël Coward
Future Indefinite	1954 – Estate of Noël Coward
Private Lives	1930 – Estate of Noël Coward
Tonight at 8.30	1936 – Estate of Noël Coward
A Talent To Amuse	1969 – Sheridan Morley
Blithe Spirit	1942 – Estate of Noël Coward
Gertrude Lawrence	1981 – Sheridan Morley
Not Yet The Dodo	1965 – Estate of Noël Coward

DIARIES

Noël Coward Diaries   1981 – Estate of Noël Coward

All professional performance rights whatsoever in these plays are strictly reserved and application for performance etc. should be made before rehearsal to Curtis Brown, Haymarket House, 28/29 Haymarket, London SW1Y 4SP. No performance may be given unless a licence has been obtained.

All amateur performance rights whatsoever in these plays are controlled by Samuel French Limited and application for performance etc, should be made before rehearsal to Samuel French Limited, 52 Fitzroy Street, London W1P 6JR, or 45 West 25th Street, New York, NY 10010-2751. No performance may be given unless a licence has been obtained.

For all rights other than stage rights, apply to Alan Brodie Representation Ltd., 211 Piccadilly, London W1V 9LD.

This book is sold subject to condition that it shall not by way of trade or otherwise be circulated without the publishers consent in any form of binding other than that in which it is published and without a similar condition including this condition being imposed on any subsequent purchaser.

A CIP catalogue record for this book is available from the British Library.

ISBN 1 84002 022 9

Cover design: Andrzej Klimowski
Photographs of *Shadow Play* and cover photograph by SASHA of London.
Copyright Cyril Holness © 1936
Cover Typography: Richard Doust

Printed in Great Britain by Arrowhead Books Ltd, Reading

IMPORTANT BILLING AND CREDIT REQUIREMENTS

All producers of *Noël and Gertie* must give credit to Sheridan Morley as devisor of the Work, in all programmes distributed in connection with performances of the Work. In all instances in which the title of the Work appears for the purposes of advertising, publicizing or otherwise exploiting a production thereof; including, without limitation, all billboards, houseboards, posters, signs and marquees. The name of Sheridan Morley must also appear on a separate line in which no other matter appears, immediately following the title of the Work, and *must* be in size of type not less than 50% of the size of type used for the title of the work.

In all programmes distributed in connection with performances of the Work, the billing and credits page shall appear in the form shown below:

(Name of Producer)

presents

NOËL AND GERTIE

an entertainment devised by Sheridan Morley
with the words and music of Noël Coward

ACKNOWLEDGEMENTS

The extracts from the plays, letters and other writings of Noël Coward reprinted by kind permission of the estate of Noël Coward.

Author's note

This is an entertainment for two actors and a pianist, drawn from the songs, plays, letters, poems, films and diaries of Noël Coward and the biographies of Noël Coward and Gertrude Lawrence by Sheridan Morley. It first opened in this form at the Donmar Warehouse in London in 1985, and was later seen at the Comedy Theatre (with Simon Cadell and Patricia Hodge) and at the Duke of York's (with Edward Petherbridge and Susan Hampshire). Subsequently, it has been seen on several British and European tours, and had its American premiere at the York Theatre, New York in December 1992 with Michael Zaslow and Jane Summerhays.

The most recent production, at the Mill at Sonning in Berkshire and the Jermyn Street Theatre in London, 1997, starred Peter Land and Elizabeth Counsell, and was directed by Sheridan Morley with choreography by Irving Davies.

For Patricia Hodge, who made my
dream a reality, with all my love

SM

PHOTO: SASHA of London

Noël Coward and Gertrude Lawrence in *Shadow Play*.

PREFACE

They were the first of the Beautiful People, and also perhaps the last of them; they looked rich and were elegant; they sang, they danced, they made jokes through clenched cigarette holders. They were impeccable. Their only true rivals, now, then or ever, were Fred and Ginger and they, after all, were only celluloid. Noël and Gertie, for six short years from 1930, were real. It was all a very long time ago, and one of the most remarkable things about that legendary partnership is that its enduring fame rests on only two productions, *Private Lives* in 1930 and *Tonight at 8.30* in 1936, neither of which they played for more than twelve weeks in London and twelve in New York. But they had of course been friends and even colleagues for rather longer than that. Both had come from similar backgrounds; not, as is now widely believed, the background of country-house parties and yachts that their stage presence was always to conjure up, but instead South London backgrounds of genteel poverty. Gertrude Lawrence, ever a romantic, was later to give colourful if fictional accounts of herself dancing barefoot outside Edwardian pubs. Noël was always more careful to separate his truth from her fiction.

"I was born in Teddington, Middlesex, an ordinary middle-class little boy. I did not gnaw kippers' heads in the gutter as Gertie quite untruthfully insisted that she did, but nor was my first memory the crunch of carriage wheels in the drive. Because we hadn't got a drive." They first met on Euston Station in 1913. He was 13, she 14, and they were on their way to Liverpool to appear in a Basil Dean production of *Hannele*.

"She wore a black satin coat," wrote Noël later, "and a black velvet military hat with a peak. Her face was far from pretty but tremendously alive. She was very 'mondaine', carried a hand-bag with a powder-puff and frequently dabbed at her generously turned-up nose. She confided to me that her name was Gertrude Lawrence but that I was to call her Gert because everybody did. She then gave me an orange, told me a few mildly dirty stories and I loved her from that moment onwards."

After *Hannele* they went their separate professional ways for almost a decade. Then, in 1923, he wrote a revue called *London Calling* and she was already its star. *Parisian Pierrot* which he composed and she sang, was their first great hit but ironically it was the success given to Gertie by Noël with that one number which took her again out of his orbit and on to Broadway, where she was to spend the rest of the 1920's while he, back in London, wrote a succession of straight hits from *The Vortex* to *Hay Fever*.

Occasionally, however, they would still meet, dance and talk of the day when they could work together again. He promised her a musical, but when it became clear to him that *Bitter Sweet* was outside her ever-limited vocal range, his thoughts turned towards a comedy, one which eventually came to him as he lay sleepless in a Tokyo hotel bedroom: "The moment I switched out the lights, Gertie appears in a white Molyneux dress on a terrace in the South of France and refused to go away again until four in the morning, by which time *Private Lives*, title and all, had constructed itself."

The rest, of course, is stage history. *Private Lives* offered its customers the second most famous balcony scene (after *Romeo and Juliet*) in all theatre and added Noël, "everything that Gertie had been in my mind when I originally conceived the play came to light on that stage – the witty, quicksilver delivery of lines, the romantic quality, tender and alluring, the swift, brittle rages... Gertie had an astounding sense of reality of the moment and her moments, dictated by the extreme variability of her moods, changed so swiftly that it was frequently difficult to discover what, apart from eating and sleeping and acting, was true of her at all."

Inspired by that variability, and the need to find another vehicle to suit them both, Noël in 1936 came up with not one but ten new plays, nine of which they eventually did in repertoire as *Tonight at 8.30*. It was a remarkably ambitious and successful solution to the very real problem of boredom that they both found in doing only one play night after night, and gave them the chance to play everything from the original *Brief Encounter* through *Hands Across the Sea* (a Mountbatten parody) and *Shadow Play* (a distant echo of their *Private Lives* relationship) to *Red Peppers*, a nostalgic mockery of the tacky music-hall tours which were a part of Gertie's if not Noël's theatrical apprenticeship.

But that, incredibly, was that. The war came, Gertie married and settled in America, and Noël continued to live and work on this side of the Atlantic always believing that there would be another chance to revive the old partnership magic. He declined the Yul Brynner role in *The King and I* however, without realising that it was to be Gertie's last appearance. She died of cancer, during the run of that show on Broadway in 1952. "I wish so very deeply," he wrote in a Times obituary the next morning, "that I could have seen her just once more in a play of mine, for no one I have ever known, however brilliant and however gifted, has contributed quite what she contributed to my work. Her quality was to me unique, and her magic imperishable."

Noël was to live on for another twenty years. How often he thought back to that balcony in the South of France, to Gertie in the long white Molyneux dress, to the potency of cheap music and the Taj Mahal by moonlight and the flatness of Norfolk, only he would ever know.

"Sometimes," he told me towards the end of his life, fully forty years on from *Private Lives*, "I would look across the stage at Gertie and she would simply take my breath away." No doubt, as they said in the play; no doubt, anywhere.

Sheridan Morley 1997

NOËL AND GERTIE was first performed at the Donmar Warehouse in July, 1985 with the following cast:

    NOËL, Lewis Fiander
    GERTIE, Patricia Hodge
    PIANIST, William Blezard

A year later it opened at the Comedy Theatre, London in a production by Alan Strachan with the following cast:

    NOËL, Simon Cadell
    GERTIE, Patricia Hodge
    PIANIST, Jonathan Cohen

PART ONE

Music Cue #1: Opening

PIANIST plays "Someday I'll Find You" *under:*

NOËL: I wish so deeply, so very deeply, that I could see her just once more playing in a play of mine; from the time we started together as child actors in Liverpool, we have been integrally part of each other's lives. No one I have ever known, however gifted or however brilliant, has contributed quite what she contributed to my work. Her quality was to me unique and her magic imperishable.

GERTIE: It was so lovely, in the beginning.

NOËL: Things never stay the same – you can't expect what was lovely then to be lovely now.

GERTIE: Why not? – Why not? Then we were happy.

NOËL: Hurry, hurry, we're going back.

GERTIE: I'm not sure that I want to. I'm not at all sure. Maybe it won't be as lovely as I think it was –

NOËL: Don't be such a fool – Grab it while you can – Grab every scrap of happiness while you can. Hurry, hurry, we're going back.

GERTIE: Play – go on playing – We must have music.

GERTIE: (*SINGS.*)

> THERE IT IS AGAIN
> THE PAST IN STORE FOR US.

NOEL *AND* GERTIE: (*SING.*)

> WAKE IN MEMORY SOME FORGOTTEN SONG
> TO BREAK THE RHYTHM DRIVING US ALONG
> AND MAKE HARMONY AGAIN A LAST ENCORE FOR US.

NOËL: (SINGS.)

>CAN'T YOU REMEMBER THE FUN WE HAD?
>TIME IS SO FLEET,
>WHY SHOULDN'T WE MEET?
>WHEN YOU'RE AWAY FROM ME DAYS ARE SAD;
>LIFE'S NOT COMPLETE,
>MY SWEET, MY SWEET.

GERTIE: (SINGS.)

>SOMEDAY I'LL FIND YOU
>MOONLIGHT BEHIND YOU,
>TRUE TO THE DREAM I AM DREAMING
>AS I DRAW NEAR YOU
>YOU'LL SMILE A LITTLE SMILE;
>FOR A LITTLE WHILE

NOËL AND GERTIE: (SING.)

>WE SHALL STAND
>HAND IN HAND.

NOËL: I must go and find Sybil.

GERTIE: I must go and find Victor.

NOËL: Well, why don't you?

GERTIE: I don't want to.

NOËL: It's shameful, shameful of us.

GERTIE: Don't; I feel terrible. Don't leave me for a minute, I shall go mad if you do. We won't talk about ourselves any more, we'll talk about outside things, anything you like, only just don't leave me until I've pulled myself together.

NOËL: Very well.

GERTIE: What have you been doing lately? During these last years?

NOËL: Travelling about. I went round the world you know, after ...

GERTIE: Yes, yes, I know: How was it?

NOËL: The world?

GERTIE: Yes.

NOËL: Oh, highly enjoyable.

GERTIE: China must be very interesting.

NOËL: Very big, China.

GERTIE: And Japan?

NOËL: Very small.

GERTIE: Did you eat shark's fins, and take your shoes off, and use chopsticks and everything?

NOËL: Practically everything.

GERTIE: And India, the burning Ghars, or Ghats, or whatever they are and the Taj Mahal. How was the Taj Mahal?

NOËL: Unbelievable, a sort of dream.

GERTIE: That was the moonlight I expect, you must have seen it in the moonlight.

NOËL: Yes, moonlight can be cruelly deceptive.

GERTIE: And it didn't look like a biscuit box, did it? I've always felt that it might.

NOËL: Darling, darling, I do love you so.

GERTIE: And I do hope you met a sacred elephant. They're lint white I believe and very, very sweet.

NOËL: I've never loved anyone else for an instant.

GERTIE: No, no you musn't, Elyot, stop.

NOËL: And you love me too, don't you? There's no doubt about it anywhere, is there?

GERTIE: No, no doubt anywhere.

NOËL: You're looking very lovely, you know, in this damned moonlight Amanda. Your skin is clear and cool, your eyes are shining, and you're growing lovelier and lovelier every second as I look at you. You don't hold any mystery for me, darling, do you mind? There isn't a particle of you that I don't know, remember and want.

GERTIE: I'm glad, my sweet.

NOËL: More than any desire anywhere, deep down in my deepest heart, I want you back again – please.

GERTIE: Don't say anymore you'll make me cry so dreadfully

(SINGS.) I'LL LEAVE YOU NEVER,

NOËL AND GERTIE: (SING.)

LOVE YOU FOR EVER,
ALL OUR PAST SORROW REDEEMING,
TRY TO MAKE IT TRUE,
SAY YOU LOVE ME TOO,
SOMEDAY I'LL FIND YOU AGAIN

NOËL: "Private Lives" was conceived in Tokyo, written in Shanghai, and first produced in London, where it opened at the new Phoenix Theatre on the Charing Cross Road on September 24th 1930. It was described in the papers variously as being ...

GERTIE: "...thin," "tenuous," "brittle," "gossamer,"

NOËL: ".. iridescent" and "delightfully daring." All of which connoted to the public mind ...

GERTIE: "...cocktails," "evening dress, "repartee"...

NOËL: ... and irreverent allusions to copulation, thereby causing a gratifying number of respectable people to queue up at the box office. There is actually more to the play than this, however, but on the whole not very much. Fortunately for me I had the inestimable advantage of playing it with Gertrude Lawrence, and so three-quarters of the battle was won before the curtain went up. Everything she had been in my mind when I originally conceived the idea came to life on the stage: the witty, quick-silver delivery of the lines; the romantic quality, tender and alluring; the swift, brittle rages ...

... even the white Molyneux dress.

I would look across the stage at Gertie and she would simply take my breath away.

GERTIE: Ever since I played "Private Lives" people have been confusing me with the heroine of Noël's play. They think I must be brittle, irresponsible, and have the emotional stability of a shuttle-cock. The play also irreversibly linked me in the public eye with Noël, although we'd been linked in our own lives for much longer. But now we were:

NOËL *AND* GERTIE: (*SING.*) NOËL AND GERTIE

NOËL: I was born in Teddington, Middlesex on December 16th 1899.

GERTIE: Just before Christmas – hence the Noël. I was born, suitably enough, on Independence Day, July 4th 1901.

NOËL: She was born in 1898, only took to giving the later date in most reference books.

GERTIE: I was christened Gertrude Alexandra Dagmar Lawrence Klasen.

NOËL: We all have our problems.

I was an ordinary, middle-class little boy. I was not gutter. I didn't gnaw kippers' heads in the street as Gertie quite untruthfully always insisted she did. But nor was my first memory the crunch of carriage wheels in the drive. Because we hadn't got a drive.

GERTIE: I was called Klasen because my father was Danish, though he seemed to have come over from Schleswig Holstein to London when he was two. He became quite famous on the Halls as a Basso Profundo. His professional name was Arthur Lawrence.

NOËL: He rendered such favourites as "Nellie Dean" and "Asleep in the Deep," and his drinking song was famous throughout Brixton and Shepherd's Bush.

GERTIE: As was his drinking, and Mother left him soon after I was born. I was an only child. I can remember ...

NOËL: I can remember.

I can remember

GERTIE: By the time that Noël was ten and I was eight ...

NOËL: Eleven.

GERTIE: We had but one thought – to get onto the professional stage. For years we had been singing in public concerts at school, recitals in church –

NOËL: It was a constant source of irritation that, when I had soared magnificently through "Oh for the Wings of a Dove!", the entire congregation would shuffle onto its knees murmuring gloomy "Amens," instead of clapping loudly and shouting "Bravo!"

GERTIE: We sang at seaside talent contests.

NOËL: I also danced – violently.

GERTIE: I won a large gold sovereign.

NOËL: I won a large box of chocolates – three parts of which were wood shavings.

GERTIE: And the fortune tellers prophesied:

NOËL: "He will have a wonderful career!"

GERTIE: "A star danced and under that was I born."

NOËL: And we both fell in love with that strange, lost, innocent world of the seaside concert party.

Music Cue #2: Any Little Fish

NOËL *AND* GERTIE: (*SING.*)

> ANY LITTLE FISH CAN SWIM, ANY LITTLE BIRD CAN FLY,
> ANY LITTLE DOG AND ANY LITTLE CAT
> CAN DO A BIT OF THIS AND JUST A BIT OF THAT;
> ANY LITTLE HORSE CAN NEIGH, AND ANY LITTLE COW CAN MOO,
> BUT I CAN'T DO ANYTHING AT ALL
> BUT JUST LOVE YOU.

NOËL:

> I can remember, I can remember,
> The months of November and December.
> Were filled for me with peculiar joys
> So different from those of other boys
> For other boys would be counting the days
> Until end of term and holiday time
> But I was acting in Christmas plays
> While they were taken to pantomimes.
> I didn't envy their Eton suits,
> Their children's dances and Christmas trees.
> My life had wonderful substitutes
> For such conventional treats as these.
> I didn't envy their country larks,
> Their organised games in panelled halls;
> While they made snow men in stately parks
> I was counting the curtain calls.

GERTIE:

> I remember the auditions, the nerve-racking auditions;
> Darkened auditorium and empty, dusty stage,
> Little girls in ballet dresses practising "positions"

> Gentlemen with pince-nez asking you your age.
> Hopefulness and nervousness struggling within you,
> Dreading the familiar phrase,

NOËL: "Thank you dear, no more."

GERTIE:

> Straining every muscle, every tendon, every sinew
> To do your dance much better than you'd ever done before.
> Think of your performance. Never mind the others,
> Never mind the pianist, talent must prevail.
> Never mind the baleful eyes of other children's mothers
> Glaring from the corners and willing you to fail.

NOËL: Ah those first rehearsals!

GERTIE: Only very few lines:

NOËL: Rushing home to mother, learning them by heart,

GERTIE: "Enter left through window" –

NOËL: Dots to mark the cue lines:

GERTIE: "Exit with the others" –

NOËL: Still it *was* a part.

> Opening performance; legs a bit unsteady,

GERTIE: Dedicated tension; shivers down my spine,

NOËL: Powder, grease and eye-black, sticks of make-up ready

GERTIE: Leichner number three and number five and number nine.

NOËL: World of strange enchantment, magic for a small boy

GERTIE: Dreaming of the future,

NOËL: Reaching for the crown,

GERTIE: Rigid in the dressing room

NOËL: Listening for the call-boy

NOËL *AND* GERTIE: "Overture Beginners" "Everybody Down!"

GERTIE: Noël made his debut as Prince Mussel in "The Goldfish – A fairy Play with a Star Cast of Wonder Children" at the Crystal Palace.

NOËL: Gertie first appeared as a Robin Redbreast in "Babes in the Wood" at Brixton.

GERTIE: And before long I was training with the legendary Italia Conti. In the Spring of 1913, Miss Conti wrote to Noël's mother offering him a three-week engagement in Liverpool and Manchester with a play called "Hannele" at a salary of two pounds a week. His mother saw him off from Euston. It was the first time he had ever been away from home alone.

NOËL: Some of the children I already knew; the others were strangers and still are with the exception of a vivacious child with ringlets to whom I took an instant fancy. She wore a black satin coat and a black velvet military cap with a peak; her face was far from pretty but tremendously alive. She was very "mondaine," carried a handbag with a powder puff, and frequently dabbed her generously turned-up nose. She confided to me that her name was Gertrude Lawrence, but that I was to call her Gertie because everybody did, and that she was fourteen, just over licensing age, that she had been in Max Reinhardt's "Miracle" at Olympia, and "Fifinella" at the Gaiety Manchester. She then gave me an orange and told me a few mildly dirty stories, and I've loved her from then onwards.

GERTIE: He was a thin, shy boy with a slight lisp – and very condescending. I was a very plain little girl, with the knack of getting myself noticed. I don't think he liked the competition. I could put up with the condescension.

What I could not have endured was to have Noël ignore me. In the play he and I were angels in long white robes, gilded wings and sanctimonious smiles. One afternoon we consumed an entire box of peppermint creams backstage, and when we went on for the heaven scene, the other celestial beings seemed to float and bob dizzily around us. I stole a glance at Noël who by now had gone positively green; presently the audience was permitted an unexpected vision of heaven in which two small angels were being violently sick.

Music Cue #3: Mrs. Worthington

NOËL: (*Sings.*)

> Don't put your daughter on the stage, Mrs Worthington;
> Don't put your daughter on the stage.
> The profession's overcrowded and the struggle's pretty tough,
> And admitting the fact,
> She's burning to act,
> That isn't quite enough.
> She has nice hands, to give the wretched girl her due
> But don't you think her bust is too developed for her age?
> I repeat, Mrs Worthington,
> Sweet Mrs Worthington,
> Don't put your daughter on the stage.
>
> Regarding yours, dear Mrs Worthington
> Of Wednesday the twenty-third.
> Although your baby may be
> Keen on a stage career,
> How can I make it clear
> That this is not a good idea?
> For her to hope, dear Mrs Worthington,
> Is on the face of it absurd.
> Her personality is not in reality
> Inviting enough, exciting enough
> For this particular sphere.

DON'T PUT YOUR DAUGHTER ON THE STAGE, MRS
    WORTHINGTON;
DON'T PUT YOUR DAUGHTER ON THE STAGE.
SHE'S A BIT OF AN UGLY DUCKLING YOU MUST HONESTLY CONFESS,
AND THE WIDTH OF HER SEAT
WOULD SURELY DEFEAT
HER CHANCES OF SUCCESS.
IT'S A LOUD VOICE, AND THOUGH IT'S NOT EXACTLY FLAT
SHE'LL NEED A LITTLE MORE THAN THAT TO EARN A LIVING WAGE
ON MY KNEES, MRS WORTHINGTON,
PLEASE, MRS WORTHINGTON,
DON'T PUT YOUR DAUGHTER ON THE STAGE.

DON'T PUT YOUR DAUGHTER ON THE STAGE, MRS
    WORTHINGTON;
DON'T PUT YOUR DAUGHTER ON THE STAGE.
THOUGH THEY SAID AT THE SCHOOL OF ACTING SHE WAS
    LOVELY AS PEER GYNT,
I'M AFRAID ON THE WHOLE
AN INGENUE ROLE
WOULD EMPHASIZE HER SQUINT.
SHE'S A BIG GIRL, AND THOUGH HER TEETH ARE FAIRLY GOOD
SHE'S NOT THE TYPE I EVER WOULD BE EAGER TO ENGAGE.
NO MORE BUTS, MRS WORTHINGTON,
NUTS, MRS WORTHINGTON,
DON'T PUT YOUR DAUGHTER ON THE STAGE.

DON'T PUT YOUR DAUGHTER ON THE STAGE, MRS
    WORTHINGTON;
DON'T PUT YOUR DAUGHTER ON THE STAGE.
ONE LOOK AT HER BANDY LEGS SHOULD PROVE SHE HASN'T
    GOT A CHANCE,
IN ADDITION TO WHICH
THE SON OF A BITCH
CAN NEITHER SING NOR DANCE.
SHE'S A VILE GIRL AND UGLIER THAN MORTAL SIN,
ONE LOOK AT HER HAS PUT ME IN A TEARING BLOODY RAGE
THAT SUFFICED MRS WORTHINGTON;
CHRIST, MRS WORTHINGTON,
DON'T PUT YOUR DAUGHTER ON THE STAGE.

PIANIST plays "Touring Days" *under:*

Music Cue #4: Touring Days

GERTIE: It was ten years before we worked together again. I'd toured for years as a chorus girl/understudy.

NOËL: For me, an endless succession of juveniles in the relative respectability of plays like "Peter Pan" and "Charley's Aunt."

GERTIE: Far from London, working out a terrible apprenticeship on the road – early train calls, freezing digs and dragon landladies ...

NOËL AND GERTIE: (*Sing.*)

> TOURING DAYS, TOURING DAYS,
> WHAT AGES IT SEEMS TO BE –
> SINCE THE LANDLADY AT NORWICH
> SERVED A MOUSE UP IN THE PORRIDGE,
> AND A BEETLE IN THE MORNING TEA
>
> TOURING DAYS, ALLURING DAYS,
> FAR BACK INTO THE PAST WE GAZE –

NOËL: (*Sings.*)

> WE USED TO TIP THE DRESSERS EVERY FRIDAY NIGHT,

GERTIE: (*Sings.*)

> AND PASSED IT OVER LIGHTLY WHEN THEY CAME IN TIGHT,

NOËL AND GERTIE: (*Sing.*)

> BUT SOMEHOW TO US IT SEEMED ALRIGHT,
> THOSE WONDERFUL TOURING DAYS.

NOËL: In between the matinee and evening performance the stage had an even greater allure for me; with only a few working lights left on here and there, it appeared vaster and more mysterious, like an empty, echoing cathedral smelling faintly of dust. Sometimes the safety curtain was not lowered, and I used to stand down on the edge of the footlights singing shrilly into the shadowy auditorium.

GERTIE: Well before he was twenty, Noël was not only an actor but also a writer. Songs, sketches and plays were pouring out of him. He was hailed as "The Young Playwright of Great Promise."

NOËL: I was a "young playwright of great promise" from 1920 until well into the Thirties, but after that the mirage faded and all hope died. It is true that during that period I wrote "The Vortex," "Bitter Sweet," "Private Lives," "Cavalcade" and several other plays, but the critical laurels so confidently prophesied for me never graced my brow and I was forced to console myself with the bitter palliative of commercial success, which I enjoyed very much indeed.

GERTIE: In 1922, he was invited to write a revue for the leading impresario, Andre Charlot, whose smart new intimate word and music shows were the rage of fashionable London, and for whom I'd been working for the past eight years.

NOËL: Gertie had realised every understudy's dream – she'd gone on for the star, Beatrice Lillie, and made her name. She'd also married Charlot's stage manager, borne him a daughter – her only child – one Saturday night after the show, and left him.

She'd also been sacked, at least twice, for unprofessional behaviour, made a fresh name for herself as a night club singer, and been taken back again.

The title of Charlot's 1922 revue was "London Calling," named after the new BBC Radio call-sign. When I was on a visit to a nightclub in Berlin a frowsy blonde, wearing a sequin chest-protector and a divided skirt, appeared in the course of the cabaret with a rag pierrot doll dressed in black satin. She placed it on a cushion where it sprawled in pathetic abandon while she pranced around it emitting guttural noises. Her performance was unimpressive, but the doll fascinated me. A title slipped into my mind, and in the taxi on the way back to the hotel the song began. It was the first one I wrote specially for Gertie.

Music Cue #5: Parisian Pierrot

GERTIE: (SINGS.)

FANTASY IN OLDEN DAYS
IN VARYING AND DIFFERENT WAYS,
WAS VERY MUCH IN VOGUE;
COLUMBINE AND PANTALOON,
A WISTFUL PIERROT 'NEATH THE MOON,
AND HARLEQUIN A ROGUE.

NOWADAYS PARISIANS OF LEISURE
WAKE THE ECHO OF AN OLD REFRAIN,
EACH SOME RAGGED EFFIGY WILL TREASURE FOR HIS PLEASURE,
TILL THE SHADOWS OF THEIR STORY LIVE AGAIN.

PARISIAN PIERROT,
SOCIETY'S HERO,
THE LORD OF A DAY,
THE RUE DE LA PAIX,
IS UNDER YOUR SWAY.
THE WORLD MAY FLATTER,
BUT WHAT DOES THAT MATTER,
THEY'LL NEVER SHATTER YOUR GLOOM PROFOUND.

PARISIAN PIERROT,
YOUR SPIRIT'S AT ZERO,
DIVINELY FORLORN
WITH EXQUISITE SCORN
FROM SUN-SET TO DAWN.
THE LIMBO IS CALLING,
YOUR STAR WILL BE FALLING,
AS SOON AS THE CLOCK GOES ROUND,
AS SOON AS THE CLOCK GOES ROUND.

NOËL: I cannot offhand think of anyone who was more intimately and turbulently connected with our theatres in the 20s than myself. Except possibly Gertie. And for me, with success came many pleasurable trappings. A car. New suits. Silk shirts, and extravagant amount of pyjamas and dressing gowns and a still more extravagant amount of publicity. I was photographed and interviewed and photographed again. In the street. In the park. In my dressing room. At my piano. With my dear old mother, without my dear old mother, and on one occasion sitting up in an over-elaborate bed looking like a heavily doped Chinese illusionist. Now, I am neither stupid nor scared, and my sense of my own importance to the world is relatively small. On the other hand, my sense of my own importance to myself is tremendous. I am all I have, to work with, to play with, to suffer and enjoy. It's not the eyes of others I am wary of, but my own. I do not intend to let myself down more than I can possibly help, and I find the fewer illusions I have about me or the world around me, the better company I am for myself.

GERTIE: In 1929 I was on Broadway in a play called "Candle-Light." It was my first appearance in America in a serious play rather than a musical, and I was both excited and terrified. On the first night I had a cable from Noël, who was, as usual, going round the world on a tramp steamer.

NOËL: LEGITIMATE AT LAST. WON'T MOTHER BE PLEASED.

GERTIE: Unfortunately my contract for "Candle-Light" prevented me from creating the role of Sari in Noël's new musical play "Bitter Sweet" which he had written with me in mind.

NOËL: Never mind darling, I'll writer another play specially for us, that will be even better.

Originally I started on the score of "Bitter Sweet" with Gertie in mind, but when it was almost done, she and I both realized that her voice, although high and charming, was not strong enough to carry such a heavy singing role. She was naturally disappointed and I promised the next play I wrote would be specially for her.

GERTIE: One night, when he was leaving New York to travel round the world – yet again – I gave him a party and a going away present, a little gold book from Cartier, which opened to reveal on one side a clock, and on the other an extremely pensive photograph of me.

NOËL: I gazed daily, with growing irritation, at that anxious, retroussé face while my mind voyaged barrenly through eighteenth-century salons, second empire drawing-rooms and modern cocktail bars in search of some slight thread of plot that might suitably unite us. None appeared, and I swore never again to promise a play for anyone in particular. I would write whatever the spirit moved me to write, regardless of whether the subject suited Gertie, Mrs. Pat Campbell or Grock.

GERTIE: But you didn't promise either of them a comedy, you promised me one.

NOËL: Promises can be broken, you know, especially if you persist in thinking of me as your pet dramatist.

GERTIE: You're a pompous ass.

NOËL: I beg you pardon?

GERTIE: I said you're a pompous ass. Anyway there are other writers you know: maybe I should go find some of them.

NOËL: God help the poor darlings if you do.

GERTIE: God has always been very good to me (so there). A pity the same can't be said about you.

NOËL: I was in Tokyo, in bed, trying to get an early night, but the moment I switched out the lights Gertie appeared in a white Molyneux dress on a terrace and refused to go away until four in the morning by which time *Private Lives* title and all had constructed itself. By the time I got to Shanghai I was able to cable Gertie in New York telling her to keep herself free for the fall.

There followed a tremendous transatlantic telegraphic bickering.

GERTIE: HAVE READ YOUR PLAY NOTHING WRONG THAT CAN'T BE FIXED.

NOËL: THE ONLY THING NEEDING TO BE FIXED WILL BE YOUR PERFORMANCE.

GERTIE: I MEANT FIXING MY CONTRACT WITH CHARLOT STOP CAN WE OPEN IN JANUARY INSTEAD OF SEPTEMBER?

NOËL: NO.

GERTIE: IN THAT CASE CAN YOU APPEAR IN CHARLOT'S REVUE WITH ME JUST TO FILL IN?

NOËL: NO.

GERTIE: IN THAT CASE COULD YOU WIRE CHARLOT ASKING HIM TO RELEASE ME FROM MY CONTRACT?

NOËL: NO.

GERTIE: NEVER MIND IT WASN'T A CONTRACT AT ALL. JUST A MORAL OBLIGATION.

NOËL: GOOD.

GERTIE: WELL ACTUALLY IT WAS A CONTRACT BUT MY LAWYERS ARE WORKING NIGHT AND DAY TO GET ME OUT OF IT.

NOËL: GOOD.

GERTIE: BY THE WAY, WOULD YOU LIKE MY CABLE ADDRESS?

NOËL: It would have saved me about forty-five pounds.

GERTIE: Maybe I won't be able to do your play at all.

NOËL: Then I shall find someone else.

GERTIE: When do we start rehearsing?

> *PIANIST starts to play* "Someday I'll Find You."
>
> *Music Cue #6: Someday I'll Find You*

NOËL: In "Private Lives" I played Elyot Chase...

GERTIE: And I played Amanda Prynne...

NOËL: A divorced couple who suddenly finds themselves on adjacent balconies at a hotel in the south of France, whilst on honeymoon with their respective spouses.

GERTIE: The other two parts were played by Adrianne Allen and a young Laurence Olivier.

NOËL: We were fortunate. The other roles are little better than ninepins, and only there at all in order to be repeatedly knocked down and stood up again by Elyot and Amanda.

GERTIE: Thoughtful of them to play that, wasn't it?

NOËL: (*In a stifled voice.*) What are you doing here?

GERTIE: I'm on honeymoon.

NOËL: How interesting, so am I.

GERTIE: I hope you're enjoying it.

NOËL: It hasn't started yet.

GERTIE: Neither has mine.

NOËL: Oh my God.

GERTIE: I can't help feeling this is a little unfortunate.

NOËL: Are you happy?

GERTIE: Perfectly.

NOËL: Good. That's all right then, isn't it?

GERTIE: Are you?

NOËL: Ecstatically.

GERTIE: What are we to do?

NOËL: I don't know.

GERTIE: Whose yacht is that?

NOËL: The Duke of Westminster's I expect. It always is.

GERTIE: I wish I were on it.

NOËL: I wish you were too.

GERTIE: There's no need to be nasty.

NOËL: Yes, there is every need. I've never in my life felt a greater urge to be nasty.

GERTIE: And you've had some urges in your time haven't you?

NOËL: If you start bickering with me, Amanda, I swear I'll throw you over the edge.

GERTIE: Try it, that's all, just try it.

NOËL: You've upset everything, as usual.

GERTIE: I've upset everything!! What about you?

NOËL: Ever since the first moment I was unlucky enough to set eyes on you, my life has been insupportable.

GERTIE: Oh do shut up, there's no sense in going on like that.

NOËL: Nothing's any use. There's no escape, ever.

GERTIE: Don't be so melodramatic.

NOËL: Do you want a cocktail? There are two here.

GERTIE: There are two over here as well.

NOËL: We'll have my two first.

GERTIE: Shall we get roaring screaming drunk?

NOËL: I don't think that would help, we did it once before and it was a dismal failure.

GERTIE: It was lovely at the beginning.

NOËL: You have an immoral memory Amanda. Here's to you.

They raise their glasses.

GERTIE: I tried to get away the moment after I'd seen you, but he wouldn't budge.

NOËL: What's his name?

GERTIE: Victor, Victor Prynne.

NOËL: Mr and Mrs Victor Prynne. Mine wouldn't budge either.

GERTIE: What's her name?

NOËL: Sybil.

GERTIE: Mr and Mrs. Elyot Chase. God pity the poor girl.

NOËL: Are you in love with him?

GERTIE: Of course.

NOËL: How funny.

GERTIE: I don't see anything particularly funny about it, you're in love with yours aren't you?

NOËL: Certainly.

GERTIE: There you are then.

NOËL: There we both are then.

GERTIE: What's she like?

NOËL: Fair, very pretty, plays the piano beautifully.

GERTIE: Very comforting.

NOËL: How's yours?

GERTIE: I'd rather not discuss him, if you don't mind.

NOËL: Well, it doesn't matter, he'll probably come popping out in a minute and I shall see for myself. Does he know I'm here?

GERTIE: Yes, I told him.

NOËL: (*Sarcastically.*) That's going to make things a whole lot easier.

GERTIE: You needn't be frightened, he won't hurt you.

NOËL: If he comes near me, I'll scream the place down.

GERTIE: What's happened to yours?

NOËL: Didn't you hear her screaming? She's downstairs in the dining room I think.

GERTIE: Mine is being grand, in the bar.

NOËL: It really is awfully difficult.

GERTIE: Have you known her long?

NOËL: About four months, we met at a house party in Norfolk.

GERTIE: Very flat, Norfolk.

NOËL: And how old is dear Victor?

GERTIE: Thirty-four, or five; and Sybil?

NOËL: I blush to tell you, only twenty-three.

GERTIE: You've gone a mucker alright.

NOËL: I shall reserve my opinion of your choice until I've met dear Victor.

GERTIE: I do wish you wouldn't go on calling him "dear Victor." It's extremely irritating.

NOËL: That's how I see him. Dumpy and fair, and very considerate, with glasses. Dear Victor.

GERTIE: As I said before, I would rather not discuss him. At least I have good taste enough to refrain from making cheap gibes at Sybil.

NOËL: You said Norfolk was flat.

GERTIE: That was no reflection on her, unless of course she made it flatter.

NOËL: Your voice takes on an acid quality whenever you mention her name.

GERTIE: I swear I'll never mention it again.

NOËL: Good, and I'll keep off yours.

GERTIE: Thank you.

NOËL: That pianist seems to have a remarkably small repertoire.

GERTIE: He doesn't seem to know anything but this, does he?

Slight pause while THEY listen to the music. She sings "Someday I'll Find You".

NOËL: You always had a sweet voice, Amanda.

GERTIE: Thank you.

NOËL: I'm awfully sorry about all this, really I am. I wouldn't have had it happen for the world.

GERTIE: I know. I'm sorry too. It's just rotten luck.

NOËL: I'll go away tomorrow whatever happens, so don't you worry.

GERTIE: That's nice of you.

NOËL: I hope everything turns out splendidly for you, and that you'll be very happy.

GERTIE: I hope the same for you too.

The PIANIST strikes up "Someday I'll Find You" *once again – brightly.*

NOËL: Nasty, insistent little tune.

GERTIE: Strange how potent cheap music is.

Pause.

NOËL: What exactly were you remembering at that moment?

GERTIE: The Palace Hotel Skating Rink in the morning, bright strong sunlight and everybody whirling round in vivid colours, and you kneeling down to put my skates on for me.

NOËL: You'd fallen on your fanny a few moments before.

GERTIE: It was beastly of you to laugh like that. I felt so humiliated.

NOËL: Poor darling.

GERTIE: Do you remember waking up in the morning, and standing on the balcony, looking out across the valley?

NOËL: Blue shadows on white snow, cleanness beyond belief, high above everything in the world. How beautiful it was.

GERTIE: It's nice to think we had a few marvellous moments.

NOËL: A few? We had heaps, really, only they slip away into the background and one only remembers the bad ones.

GERTIE: Yes. What fools we were to ruin it all. What utter, utter, fools.

NOËL: You feel like that too, do you?

GERTIE: Of course.

NOËL: Why did we?

GERTIE: The whole business was too much for us.

NOËL: We were so ridiculously over in love.

GERTIE: Funny, wasn't it?

NOËL: Horribly funny.

GERTIE: Selfishness, cruelty, hatred, petty jealousy. All those qualities came out in us just because we loved each other.

NOËL: Perhaps they were there anyhow.

GERTIE: No, it's love that does it. To hell with love!

NOËL: To hell with love!!

Playout.

GERTIE: We played a short provincial tour of "Private Lives" before bringing it to London. By now we were swathed in luxury – the touring days of the past belonging to another world.

NOËL: Assurance of success seemed to be emblazoned on the play from the first. We had few qualms, played to capacity business and enjoyed ourselves thoroughly. We felt, I think rightly, that there was a shine on us.

GERTIE: In London we were an immediate hit, and our three months' limited engagement was sold out during the first week.

NOËL: One night Mrs. Patrick Campbell swept into my dressing room in a state of some agitation.

GERTIE: (*Sweepingly.*) "Your characters all talk like typewriters. But I do so like it when you do your little hummings at the piano."

NOËL: We closed, at the end of our three scheduled months, with the gratifying knowledge that we could have easily run on for another six. The phenomenon was then repeated in New York. For Gertie this was the climax of a glittering six years on Broadway, a whirling dream!

Music Cue #7: Dance, Little Lady

NOËL: (*SINGS.*)

DANCE, DANCE, DANCE, LITTLE LADY,
YOUTH IS FLEETING – TO THE RHYTHM BEATING
IN YOUR MIND
DANCE, DANCE, DANCE LITTLE LADY.
SO OBSESSED WITH SECOND BEST,
NO REST YOU'LL EVER FIND,
TIME AND TIDE AND TROUBLE
NEVER, NEVER WAIT.
LET THE CAULDRON BUBBLE
JUSTIFY YOUR FATE.
DANCE, DANCE, DANCE LITTLE LADY
DANCE, DANCE, DANCE, LITTLE LADY
LEAVE TOMORROW BEHIND.

PIANIST continues playing under.

NOËL: Gertie has an astounding sense of the reality of the moment, and her moments, dictated by the extreme variability of her moods, change so swiftly that it is frequently difficult to discover what (apart from eating and sleeping and acting) is true of her at all. I know her better, I believe, than most people. The early years of our friendship set her strongly in my mind; I knew her then to have quick humour, insane generosity and a loving heart and those things seldom change. I see her now, ages away from her ringlets and black military cap, sometimes a wide-eyed child, sometimes a glamorous femme du monde, at some moments a rather boisterous good sort and at others a weary disillusioned woman battered by life but gallant to the last. In adolescence she was barely pretty; now, without apparent effort, she gives the impression of sheer loveliness. On stage she is potentially capable of anything and everything; she can play a scene one night with perfect subtlety and the next with such vulgarity that your senses reel. She has in abundance every theatrical essential except one; critical faculty.

GERTIE: He used to say that not only did I never play a scene the same two nights running, but he couldn't be sure what I'd do the third night either. Nobody ever could, not even me.

NOËL *AND* GERTIE: (*SING.*)

> WHEN THE SAXOPHONE
> GIVES A WICKED MOAN,
> CHARLESTON HEY HEY,
> RHYTHMS FALL AND RISE,
> START DANCING TO THE TUNE,
> THE BAND'S CROONING –
> FOR SOON THE NIGHT WILL BE GONE
> START SWAYING LIKE A REED
> WITHOUT HEEDING THE SPEED
> THAT HURRIES YOU ON.
> SYNCOPATE YOUR NERVES
> TILL YOUR BODY CURVES
> DROOPING – STOOPING,
> LAUGHTER SOME DAY DIES,
> AND WHEN THE LIGHTS ARE STARTING TO GUTTER
> DAWN THROUGH THE SHUTTER
> SHOWS YOU'RE LIVING A WORLD OF LIES.

NOËL: (*SINGS.*)

> DANCE, DANCE, DANCE LITTLE LADY,
> YOUTH IS FLEETING – TO THE RHYTHM BEATING

IN YOUR MIND.
DANCE, DANCE, DANCE LITTLE LADY,
SO OBSESSED WITH SECOND BEST,
NO REST YOU'LL EVER FIND,
TIME AND TIDE AND TROUBLE.
NEVER, NEVER WAIT,
LET THE CAULDRON BUBBLE
JUSTIFY YOUR FATE.
DANCE, DANCE, DANCE LITTLE LADY
DANCE, DANCE, DANCE LITTLE LADY,
LEAVE TOMORROW BEHIND

(*Spoken.*) Gertie began to get the idea that money flowed in without restrictions.

GERTIE: When I remembered how hard I worked to earn fifteen shillings a week in the theatre just ten years back, it seemed incredible that I should be earning thirty-five hundred dollars a week on Broadway. Not to mention my paper profits on the market. Of course I had no idea of it at the time, but I was to be one of the victims of the Crash.

NOËL: She was spending money like an entire fleet of drunken sailors.

GERTIE: I grabbed desperately at plays, films. I opened a florist's shop.

NOËL: And still the debts mounted.

All she would say was:

GERTIE: Someone will have to do something about it.

NOËL: Gertie's managers asked me if I would consent to speak to her sharply about her extravagance.

GERTIE: They arranged a meeting.

NOËL: She will arrive in one of three moods. Either she'll be very angry and break all the furniture, or she'll be very tearful and make it all wringing wet, or else she'll just sit there with her hands on her lap and say that she doesn't understand. I only hope to God she doesn't understand.

Pause.

NOËL: In the event, she failed to turn up at all, and within a few months there were full-page press reports of her bankruptcy hearings.

GERTIE: When I came out of the Court, I had nothing, but the clothes I stood in. My cars, my house, my jewellery, had been seized. I had literally not a roof to crawl under.

NOËL: The success we had with "Private Lives" both in London and New York encouraged me to believe that the public liked to see us acting together. However, I wanted to write more than just another light comedy. I wanted to show Gertie's mercurial character and frequent changes of mood. I wanted to stop myself from being bored by playing the same thing night after night, and I wanted to make money for us both.

GERTIE: Noël darling, wouldn't three plays be better than one?

NOËL: Better than three would be nine!

GERTIE: And Gertie appeared once more at the Phoenix Theatre in:

NOËL *AND* GERTIE: "Tonight at 8.30."

Music Cue #8: Play, Orchestra, Play

NOËL *AND* GERTIE: (*SING.*)

> LISTEN TO THE STRAIN, IT PLAYS ONCE MORE FOR US.
> THERE IT IS AGAIN, THE PAST IN STORE FOR US.
> WAKE IN MEMORY SOME FORGOTTEN SONG

> To break the rhythm driving us along and make
> Harmony again, a last encore for us.
>
> Play, orchestra, play
> Play something light and sweet and gay,
> For we must have music,
> We must have music,
> To drive our fears away.
> While our illusion swiftly fade for us
> Let's have an orchestra score.
> In the confusion the years have made for us
> Serenade for us just once more
> Life needn't be grey,
> Although it's changing day by day,
> Though a few old dreams may decay,
> Play, orchestra,
> Play, orchestra,
> Play, orchestra, play!

NOËL: "Tonight at 8.30" was nine one-act plays, divided into three sets of three and played on alternate nights and matinees.

GERTIE: The strain didn't bear thinking about so we didn't. We just took a deep breath and jumped.

Music Cue #9: We Were Dancing

GERTIE: (*Sings.*)

> We were dancing
> And the gods must have found it entrancing.
> For they smiled
> On a moment undefiled
> By the care and woe that mortals know.

NOËL *and* GERTIE: (*Sing.*)

> We were dancing
> And the music and lights were enhancing
> Our desire,
> When the world caught on fire
> She and I were dancing.

NOËL: (*Sings.*)

> LOVE LAY IN WAIT FOR US,
> TWISTED OUR FATE FOR US,
> NO ONE WARNED US,
> REASON SCORNED US,
> TIME STOOD STILL
> IN THAT FIRST STRONG THRILL.

GERTIE: (*Sings.*)

> DESTINY KNEW OF US,
> GUIDED THE TWO OF US,
> HOW COULD WE REFUSE TO SEE
> THAT WRONG SEEMED RIGHT
> ON THIS LYRICAL ENCHANTED NIGHT.

She has hammed this up. NOËL glowers at her.

NOËL: Telegram to Jack Wilson's Management:

> WILL NOT APPEAR UNLESS I GET A FURTHER 58 PER CENT OF THE GROSS FOR ARDUOUS TASK OF RESTRAINING MISS LAWRENCE FROM BEING GROCK, BEATRICE LILLIE, THEDA BARA, MARY PICKFORD, AND BERT LAHR ALL AT ONCE.

GERTIE: (*Sings.*)

> LOGIC SUPPLIES NO LAWS FOR IT,
> ONLY ONE CAUSE FOR IT.

NOËL *AND* GERTIE: (*Sing.*)

> WE WERE DANCING
> AND THE MUSIC AND LIGHT WERE ENHANCING
> OUR DESIRE
> WHEN THE WORLD CAUGHT ON FIRE
> SHE AND I WERE DANCING.

NOËL: In the dream world of "Shadow Play" a husband and wife on the point of breaking up recall their first meeting.

GERTIE: It's nice and cool in the garden – country house dances can be so lovely.

NOËL: Do you know this part of the country?

GERTIE: Intimately. I'm staying here with my aunt.

NOËL: Does she ride to hounds?

GERTIE: Incessantly. She's a big woman and she kills little foxes – she's kind *au fond,* but she dearly loves killing little foxes.

NOËL: Are you engaged for this dance?

GERTIE: I was, but I'll cut it if you'll promise to love me always and never let anything or anybody spoil it – never –

NOËL: But of course – that's understood.

GERTIE: My name's Victoria – Victoria Marden.

NOËL: Mine's Simon Gayforth.

GERTIE: How do you do?

NOËL: Quite well, thank you.

GERTIE: I suppose you came down for the dance?

NOËL: Yes, I'm staying with the Bursbys –

GERTIE: What do you do?

NOËL: I'm in a bank.

GERTIE: High up in a bank? Or just sitting in a cage totting up things?

NOËL: Oh, quite high up, really – it's a very good bank.

GERTIE: I'm so glad.

NOËL: How lovely you are.

GERTIE: Small talk – a lot of small talk with quite different thoughts going on behind it – this garden's really beautiful. Are you good at gardens?

NOËL: No but I'm persevering – I'm all right on the more straightforward blooms – you know, snapdragon, sweet William, cornflowers and tobacco plant – and I can tell a Dorothy Perkins a mile off.

GERTIE: That hedge over there is called a Cupressus Macrocapa.

NOËL: Do you swear it?

GERTIE: It grows terrifically quickly but they do say that it goes a bit thin underneath in about twenty years.

NOËL: How beastly of them to say that – it's slander.

GERTIE: Did you know about Valerian smelling of cats?

NOËL: You're showing off again.

GERTIE: It's true.

NOËL: I can go one better than that – Lotuses smell of pineapples.

GERTIE: (*Sadly.*) Everything smells of something else – it's dreadfully confusing.

NOËL: Never mind darling – I love you desperately – I knew it the first second I saw you.

Music Cue #10: You Were There

NOËL: (*Sings.*)

> WAS IT IN THE REAL WORLD?
> OR WAS IT IN A DREAM?
> WAS IT JUST A NOTE IN SOME ETERNAL THEME?
> WAS IT ACCIDENTAL
> OR ACCURATELY PLANNED?
> HOW COULD I HESITATE
> KNOWING THAT MY FATE
> LED ME BY THE HAND.

NOËL *AND* GERTIE: (*Sing.*)

> YOU WERE THERE
> I SAW YOU AND MY HEART STOPPED BEATING

YOU WERE THERE
AND IN THAT FIRST ENCHANTED MEETING
LIFE CHANGED ITS TUNE, THE STARS AND MOON CAME NEAR TO ME
DREAMS THAT I DREAMED, LIKE MAGIC SEEMED TO BE CLEAR
    TO ME
DEAR TO ME;

YOU WERE THERE
YOUR EYES LOOKED INTO MINE AND FALTERED
EVERYWHERE
THE COLOUR OF THE WHOLE WORLD ALTERED.
FALSE BECAME TRUE
MY UNIVERSE TUMBLED IN TWO
THE EARTH BECAME HEAVEN FOR YOU WERE THERE.

YOU WERE THERE,
YOUR EYES LOOKED INTO MINE AND FALTERED,
EVERYWHERE
THE COLOUR OF THE WHOLE WORLD ALTERED.
FALSE BECAME TRUE
MY UNIVERSE TUMBLED IN TWO
THE EARTH BECAME HEAVEN FOR YOU WERE THERE.

Music Cue #11: Then

GERTIE: (*SINGS.*)

HERE IS THE LIGHT OF THIS UNKIND FAMILIAR NOW
EVERY GESTURE IS CLEAR AND COLD FOR US
EVEN YESTERDAY'S GROWING OLD FOR US
EVERYTHING'S CHANGED SOMEHOW.
THERE'S SOME FORGOTTEN LOVER'S VOW
COULD WAKE A MEMORY IN MY HEART AGAIN
PERHAPS THE JOY THAT WE KNEW COULD START AGAIN
CAN'T WE RECLAIM AN HOUR OR SO?
THE PAST IS NOT SO LONG AGO.

THEN, LOVE WAS COMPLETE FOR US,
THEN, THE DAYS WERE SWEET FOR US,
LIFE ROSE TO ITS FEET FOR US
AND STEPPED ASIDE BEFORE OUR PRIDE.
AH THEN, WE KNEW THE BEST OF IT,
OUR HEARTS STOOD THE TEST OF IT.

> Now the magic has flown
> We face the unknown
> Apart and alone.

NOËL: "Red Peppers" is a vaudeville sketch sandwiched between two parodies of music hall songs: Of all the nine plays, it was the one we enjoyed performing the most. It is set in a run down music-hall and starts with the equally run down comedy and song act doing their first half spot. Gertie used to say this was the sort of theatre she played in her youth, but as with the kippers' heads, she was prone to exaggerate the depths from which she had risen. Although I never played the halls myself, I've shared digs with those who did and observed them at close quarters. My respect for their professionalism and fascination with their world remains undiminished; a proud breed, now virtually extinct.

Ladies and gentlemen, with your very kind indulgence, my wife and myself would like to present you with our very famous nautical extravaganza. Ready Bert?

GERTIE: Right.

NOËL: Take it away.

Music Cues #12: Has Anybody Seen Our Ship?

NOËL: (*Sings.*)

> What shall we do with the drunken sailor?
> So the saying goes.
> We're not tight but we're none too bright
> Great Scott! I don't suppose.
> We've lost our way
> And we've lost our pay
> And to make the thing complete,
> We've been and gone and lost the blooming fleet.
>
> Has anybody seen our ship, the HMS Peculiar?
> We've been on shore for a month or more
> And when we see the captain we shall get what for.

Heave ho! Me hearties, sing glory hallelujah
A lady bold as she could be
Pinched our whistles at the golden key.
Now we're in between the devil and the deep blue sea.
Has anybody seen our ship?

La la la la la la la la la la la – Shut up, shut up, shut up ...

GERTIE: 'Ere Jack, who was that lady I saw you walking down the street with last night.

NOËL: That was no lady, that was my wife! Wait for it, wait for it ...

GERTIE: Better to come, better to come. 'Ere Jack, I've got a little riddle to ask you.

NOËL: You've got a little riddle to ask me?

GERTIE: I've got a little riddle to ask you: Why is getting up at 6 o'clock in the morning like a pig's tail?

NOËL: I don't know – why is getting up at 6 o'clock in the morning like a pig's tail?

GERTIE: Twirly.

NOËL: Oh dear, oh dear, oh dear, keep it clean, keep it fresh, keep it fragrant. 'Ere Jack.

GERTIE: Yes Jack?

NOËL: Tar! (*Laughs.*) Thank you.

Was that your dog I saw you with in the High Street?

GERTIE: Yes, that was my dog.

NOËL: What's his name?

GERTIE: Fruit Salts

NOËL: Fruit Salts? Why?

GERTIE: Ask him – 'Eno's

NOËL: Every one a winner.

GERTIE: 'Ere Jack, I've been very worried about you lately.

NOËL: Pourquoi? French.

GERTIE: I heard you had adenoids.

NOËL: You heard I had adenoids?

GERTIE: I heard you had adenoids.

NOËL: Don't speak of it. Don't speak of it.

GERTIE: Why not?

NOËL: Adenoids me ... Keep it clean ...

GERTIE: Keep it fresh.

NOËL: Keep it fragrant.

NOEL *AND* GERTIE: Every one a winner.

>   (*SING.*) WHAT'S TO BE DONE WITH GIRLS ON SHORE
>   WHO LEAD OUR TARS ASTRAY?
>   WHAT'S TO BE DONE WITH THE DRINKS GALORE
>   THAT MAKE THEM PASS AWAY?
>   WE GOT WET EARS FROM OUR FIRST FIVE BEERS,
>   AFTER THAT WE LOST CONTROL
>   AND NOW WE FIND WE'RE UP THE BLINKING POLE.
>
>   HAS ANYBODY SEEN OUR SHIP, THE HMS DISGUSTING?
>   WE'VE THREE GUNS AFT AND ANOTHER ONE FORE
>   AND THEY'VE PROMISED US A FUNNEL FOR THE NEXT WORLD WAR.
>   HEAVE HO! ME HEARTIES! THE QUARTER DECK NEEDS DUSTING
>   WE HAD A BINGE LAST CHRISTMAS YEAR,
>   NICE PLUM PUDDING AND A ROUND OF BEER,
>   BUT THE CAPTAIN PULLED HIS CRACKER AND WE CRIED, OH DEAR!
>   HAS ANYBODY SEEN OUR SHIP?
>
>   HAS ANYBODY SEEN OUR SHIP, THE HMS SUGGESTIVE?
>   SHE SAILED AWAY ACROSS THE BAY

And we haven't had a smell of her since New Year's Day.
Heave ho! Me hearties, we're getting rather restive.
We pooled our money, spent the lot,
The world forgetting, by the world forgot.
Now we haven't got a penny for the you know what.
Has anybody seen, has anybody seen, has anybody seen,
Has anybody, anybody, anybody, anybody, anybody
    seen our ship?

They make a snappy exit.

INTERVAL

PART TWO

Still in "Red Peppers". As if in encore as in pages before.

Music Cue #14: Has Anybody Seen Our Ship? – Reprise

NOËL AND GERTIE: (*Sing.*)

> HAS ANYBODY SEEN OUR SHIP?
> THE HMS SUGGESTIVE?
> SHE SAILED AWAY
> ACROSS THE BAY,
> AND WE HAVEN'T HAD A SMELL OF HER SINCE NEW YEAR'S DAY
> HEAVE HO, ME HEARTIES,
> WE'RE GETTING RATHER RESTIVE.
> WE POOLED OUR MONEY, SPENT THE LOT,
> THE WORLD FORGETTING BY THE WORLD FORGOT,
> NOW WE HAVEN'T GOT A PENNY FOR THE YOU KNOW WHAT!
> HAS ANYBODY SEEN, ANYBODY SEEN, ANYBODY SEEN,
> HAS ANYBODY, ANYBODY, ANYBODY ANYBODY ANYBODY
>   SEEN OUR SHIP?

They make a snappy exit, ruined by GERTIE dropping her telescope and having to nip back for it.

NOËL: Now then.

GERTIE: Now then what?

NOËL: (*Contemptuously.*) Now then, what!

GERTIE: I don't know what you're talking about.

NOËL: Oh you don't, don't you?

GERTIE: No I don't, so shut up.

NOËL: I suppose you don't know you mucked up the whole exit!

GERTIE: It wasn't my fault.

NOËL: Whose fault was it then, Mussolini's?

GERTIE: (*With sarcasm.*) Funny, hey?

NOËL: (*Witheringly.*) I suppose you didn't drop your prop, did you! And having dropped it, you didn't have to go back for it, leaving me to prance off all by myself.

GERTIE: The exit was too quick.

NOËL: It was the same as its always been.

GERTIE: It was too quick, I tell you, its been too quick the whole week, the whole number's too quick –

NOËL: Bert Bentley takes that number at the same tempo he's always done.

GERTIE: You and your Bert Bentley, just because he stands you a Welsh rarebit at the Queen's you think he's God Almighty.

NOËL: Bert Bentley's the finest conductor in the North of England and don't you make any mistake about it.

GERTIE: Finest conductor my foot! I suppose he thinks it's funny to see us leaping up and down the stage like a couple of greyhounds.

NOËL: If you're a greyhound I'm Fred Astaire.

GERTIE: Oh, you're Fred Astaire alright, with a bit of Pavlova thrown in – you're wonderful, you are – there's nothing you can't do, except behave like a gentleman.

NOËL: Oh, so you expect me to behave like a gentleman, do you? That's a good one coming from you.

GERTIE: Oh, shut up, you make me tired.

NOËL: I make you tired! I suppose it was me who mucked up the exit – I suppose it was me that dropped the bloody telescope!

GERTIE: (*Heated.*) Now look here, George Pepper –

NOËL: Stop George Peppering me – why can't you admit it when you're in the wrong? – You mucked up the exit – nobody else did – you did!

GERTIE: Well, what if I did? It was an accident wasn't it? I didn't do it on purpose.

NOËL: It doesn't matter how you did it or why you did it, you did it.

GERTIE: (*Screaming.*) All right, I did it!

NOËL: (*Triumphant.*) Well, don't do it again.

Pause.

GERTIE: Who's on now?

NOËL: Mabel Grace just finished.

GERTIE: She's been finished for years, as far as I'm concerned.

NOËL: What's the matter with Mabel Grace?

GERTIE: Ask the public, dear, just ask the public.

NOËL: Mabel Grace is an artist and don't you forget it – she may be a bit long in the tooth now but she's a bigger star than you'll ever be, so there!

GERTIE: You make me sick, sucking up to the topliners.

NOËL: Who sucks up to topliners?

GERTIE: You do – look at Irene Baker!

NOËL: What's the matter with Irene Baker?

GERTIE: When last heard from she was falling down drunk at the Empire, Hartlepool.

NOËL: That's a dirty lie, Irene never touches a drop till after the show and well you know it.

GERTIE: (*Contemptuously.*) Irene! It was Miss Baker this and Miss Baker that, the last time you saw her.

NOËL: That's all you know.

GERTIE: Trying to make me think you got off with her, eh? What a chance!

NOËL: Oh, shut up nagging!

GERTIE: (*Muttering.*) Irene!

NOËL: If a day ever dawns when you can time your laughs like Irene Baker does, I'll give you a nice red apple!

GERTIE: Time my laughs! That's funny. Fat lot of laughs I get when you write the gags.

NOËL: (*Grandly.*) If you're dissatisfied with your material you know what you can do with it.

GERTIE: I know what I'd like to do with it.

NOËL: You can't even do a straight walk off without balling it up.

GERTIE: Oh, we're back at that again, are we?

NOËL: Yes we are, so there!

GERTIE: (*Coming over to him.*) Now look here, just you listen to me for a minute ...

NOËL: I've been listening to you for fifteen years, one more minute won't hurt.

GERTIE: I've had about enough of this. I'm sick of you and the whole act. It's lousy anyway.

NOËL: The act was good enough for my mum and dad and its good enough for you.

GERTIE: (*With heavy sarcasm.*) Time has changed a bit since your mum and dad's day, you know. There's electric light now and telephones and a little invention called moving pictures. Nobody wants to see the "Red

Peppers" for three bob when they can see Garbo for ninepence!

NOËL: That's where you're wrong, see! We're flesh and blood we are – the public would rather see flesh and blood any day than a cheesy photograph. Put Garbo on a Saturday night in Devonport, and see what would happen to her.

GERTIE: Yes, you should know, look what happened to us.

NOËL: That wasn't Devonport, it was Southsea.

GERTIE: Well, wherever it was, the Fleet was in.

NOËL: If you think the act's so lousy it's a pity you don't rewrite some of it.

GERTIE: Tried going into St. Paul's and offering to rewrite the Bible?

NOËL: Very funny! Oh, very funny indeed! You're wasted in show business, you ought to write for Comic Cuts you ought.

GERTIE: I could think up better gags than you do at that "That wasn't a lady, that was my wife!" – "D'you mind if I smoke?" – "I don't care if you burn!" – hoary old chestnuts – they were has-beens when your grandmother fell off the high wire.

NOËL: And what, may I ask, has my grandmother got to do with it?

GERTIE: She didn't fall soon enough, that's all.

NOËL: (*Furiously.*) You shut your mouth and stop hurling insults at my family. What were you when I married you, I should like to know? One of the six Moonlight Maids – dainty songs and dances, and no bookings.

GERTIE: (*Hotly.*) When we did get bookings we got number one towns, which is more than your mum and dad ever did.

NOËL: Who wants the number one towns, anyway? You can't get a public all the year round like my mum and dad did by doing a parasol dance twice a year at the Hippodrome Manchester!

GERTIE: The Moonlight Maids was just as good an act as the Red Peppers any day, and a bloody sight more refined at that!

NOËL: You've said it. That's just what it was – refined. It was so refined it simpered itself out of the bill –

GERTIE: A bit of refinement wouldn't do any harm –

NOËL: Perhaps you would like to change the act to "Musical Moments" with me playing a flute and you sitting under a standard lamp with a cello?

PIANIST. (*Yelling.*) Red Peppers you're on.

BOTH. Oh, my gawd, we're off

NOËL: 'Ere, what's your game? Quick – got your stick?

GERTIE: What do you think this is? Scotch mist?

NOËL: Well, don't drop it.

GERTIE: No, I won't.

Music Cue #14: Men About Town

NOËL *AND* GERTIE: (*SING.*)

> WE'RE TWO CHAPS WHO FIND IT THRILLING
> TO DO THE KILLING
> WE'RE ALWAYS WILLING TO GIVE THE GIRLS A TREAT
> JUST A DRINK AT THE RITZ,
> CALL IT DOUBLE OR QUITS,
> THEN WE FEEL THE WORLD IS AT OUR FEET.
>
> TOP HATS, WITH SPATS, LOOK DIVINE ON US
> THERE'S A SHINE ON US,
> GET A LINE ON US WHEN WE COME YOUR WAY

> Gad, eleven o'clock.
> Let's pop into the Troc
> 'ere we start the business of the day.
>
> As we stroll down Picc-Piccadilly
> In the bright morning air,
> All the girls turn and stare
> We're so nonchalant and frightfully debonair
> When we chat to Rose, Maud or Lily
> You should see the way their boy friends frown
> For they know without a doubt
> That their luck's right out
> Up against a couple of men about town
>
> As we stroll down Picc-Piccadilly
> All girls say, "Who's here?
> Put your hat straight my dear,
> For it's Marmaduke and Percy Vere de Vere."
> As we doff hats each pretty filly
> Gives a wink at us and then looks down,
> For they long with all their might
> For a red hot night
> When they see a couple of men about town.

Dance break.

NOËL *and* GERTIE: (*Sing.*)

> For they long with all their might
> For a red hot night
> When they see a couple of men about town.

Music interlude.

NOËL: The most mature play of the whole "Tonight at 8:30" series was "Still Life." Later it was made into an excellent film. I am fond of both the play and the film with, as usual, a slight bias in favour of the former. The characters, I think, are true, and I can say now having reread it with detachment after so many years, that I am proud to have written it. Five of the other plays were made into films; two full-length features and one anthology of three plays, but none of them made anything like the same impression. "Still Life" takes place in the buffet at Milford Junction station. It, was re-titled for the film "Brief Encounter."

PIANIST plays theme from "Brief Encounter."

I wish I could say the music in the film were mine, but I can't.

GERTIE: Do you like milk in your tea?

NOËL: Yes, don't you?

GERTIE: Yes – fortunately.

NOËL: Station refreshments are generally a wee bit arbitrary, you know.

GERTIE: I wasn't grumbling.

NOËL: Do you ever grumble – are you ever sullen and cross and bad tempered?

GERTIE: Of course I am – at least not sullen exactly – but sometimes I get into rages.

NOËL: I can't visualise you in a rage.

GERTIE: I really don't see why you should.

NOËL: Oh, I don't know – there are signs, you know – one can usually tell –

GERTIE: Long upper lips and jaw lines and eyes close together.

NOËL: You haven't any of those things.

GERTIE: Do you feel guilty at all? I do.

NOËL: (*Smiling.*) Guilty?

GERTIE: You ought to more than me, really – you neglected your work this afternoon.

NOËL: I worked this morning – a little relaxation never did anyone any harm. Why should either of us feel guilty?

GERTIE: I don't know – a sort of instinct – as though we were letting something happen that oughtn't to happen.

NOËL: How awfully nice you are!

GERTIE: When I was a child in Cornwall – we lived in Cornwall, you know – May, that's my sister, and I used to climb out of our bedroom window on summer nights and go down to the cove and bathe. It was dreadfully cold but we felt very adventurous. I'd never have dared do it by myself, but sharing the danger made it alright that's how I feel now really.

NOËL: Have a bun – it's awfully bad for you.

GERTIE: You're laughing at me!

NOËL: Yes, a little, but I'm laughing at myself, too.

GERTIE: Why?

NOËL: For feeling a small pang when you said about feeling guilty.

GERTIE: There you are, you see!

NOËL: We haven't done anything wrong.

GERTIE: Of course we haven't.

NOËL: An accidental meeting – then another accidental meeting – then a little lunch – what could be more ordinary? More natural?

GERTIE: We're adults after all.

NOËL: I never see myself as an adult, do you?

GERTIE: (*Firmly.*) Yes, I do. I'm a respectable married woman with a husband and a home and three children.

NOËL: But there must be a part of you, deep down inside, that doesn't feel like that at all – some little spirit that still wants to climb out of the window – that still longs to splash about a bit in the dangerous sea.

GERTIE: Perhaps we none of us ever grow up entirely.

NOËL: How awfully nice you are!

GERTIE: You said that before.

NOËL: I thought perhaps you hadn't heard.

GERTIE: I heard all right.

NOËL: (*Gently.*) I'm respectable too, you know. I have a home and a wife and children and responsibilities – I also have a lot of work to do and a lot of ideals all mixed up with it.

GERTIE: What's she like?

NOËL: Madeleine?

GERTIE: Yes.

NOËL: Small, dark, rather delicate –

GERTIE: How funny! I should have thought she'd be fair.

NOËL: And your husband? What's he like?

GERTIE: Medium height, brown hair, kindly, unemotional and not delicate at all.

NOËL: You said that proudly.

GERTIE: Did I? (*She looks down.*)

NOËL: What's the matter?

GERTIE: The matter? What could be the matter?

NOËL: You suddenly went away.

GERTIE: (*Brightly.*) I thought perhaps we were being rather silly.

NOËL: Why?

GERTIE: Oh, I don't know – we are such complete strangers really.

NOËL: It's one thing to close a window, but quite another to slam it down on my fingers.

GERTIE: I'm sorry.

NOËL: Please come back again.

GERTIE: Is tea bad for one? Worse than coffee, I mean?

NOËL: If this is a professional interview, my fee is a guinea.

GERTIE: (*Laughing.*) It's nearly time for your train.

NOËL: I hate to think of it, chugging along, interrupting our tea party.

GERTIE: I really am sorry now.

NOËL: What for?

GERTIE: For being disagreeable.

NOËL: I don't think you could be disagreeable.

GERTIE: You said something just now about your work and ideals being mixed up with it – what ideals?

NOËL: That's a long story.

GERTIE: I suppose all doctors ought to have ideals really, otherwise I would think the work would be unbearable.

NOËL: Surely you're not encourage me to talk shop?

GERTIE: Do you come here every Thursday?

NOËL: Yes, I come in from Churley and spend a day in the hospital. It gives me a chance to observe and study the patients.

GERTIE: Is that a great advantage?

NOËL: Of course. You see I have a special pigeon.

GERTIE: What is it?

NOËL: Preventive medicine.

GERTIE: Oh, I see.

NOËL: (*Laughing.*) I'm afraid you don't.

GERTIE: I was trying to be intelligent.

NOËL: Most good doctors, especially when they're young, have private dreams – that's the best part of them, sometimes though, those get over professionalised and strangulated and – am I boring you?

GERTIE: No – I don't quite understand – but you're not boring me.

NOËL: What I mean is this – all good doctors must be primarily enthusiasts. Must have, like writers and painters, and priests a sense of vocation, a deep rooted unsentimental desire to do good.

GERTIE: Yes, – I see that.

NOËL: Well, obviously one way of preventing disease is worth fifty ways curing it – that's where my ideal comes in – preventive medicine isn't anything to do with medicine at all, really – it's concerned with conditions, living conditions and common-sense and hygiene. For example my speciality is pneumoconiosis.

GERTIE: Oh, dear!

NOËL: Don't be alarmed, it's simpler than it sounds – it's nothing but a slow process of fibrosis of the lung due to the inhalation of particles of dust. In the hospital there are splendid opportunities for observing cures and making notes, because of the coal mine.

GERTIE: You suddenly look much younger.

NOËL: (*Brought up short.*) Do I?

GERTIE: Almost like a little boy.

NOËL: What made you say that?

GERTIE: (*Staring at him.*) I don't know – yes, I do.

NOËL: (*Gently.*) Tell me.

GERTIE: (*With panic in her voice.*) Oh, no, I couldn't, really. You were saying about the coal mine –

NOËL: (*Looking into her eyes.*) Yes – the inhalation of coal dust – that's one specific form of the disease – its called Anthracosis.

GERTIE: (*Hypnotised.*) What are the others?

NOËL: Chalicosis – that comes from metal dust-steel works, you know –

GERTIE: Yes, of course. Steel works.

NOËL: And silicosis – stone dust – that's gold mines.

GERTIE: (*Almost in a whisper.*) I see.

There is a sound of a bell.

GERTIE: That's your train.

NOËL: (*Looking down.*) Yes.

GERTIE: You musn't miss it.

NOËL: No.

GERTIE: (*Again the panic in her voice.*) What's the matter?

NOËL: (*With an effort.*) Nothing – nothing at all.

GERTIE: (*Socially.*) It's been so very nice – I've enjoyed my afternoon enormously.

NOËL: I'm so glad – so have I. I apologise for boring you with those long medical words –

GERTIE: I feel dull and stupid, not to be able to understand more.

NOËL: Shall I see you again?

GERTIE: It's the other platform, isn't it? You'll have to run. Don't worry about me – mine's due in a few minutes.

NOËL: Shall I see you again?

GERTIE: Of course – perhaps you could come over to Ketchworth one Sunday. It's rather far, I know, but we should be delighted to see you.

NOËL: (*Intensely.*) Please – please –

GERTIE: What is it?

NOËL: Next Thursday – the same time –

GERTIE: No – I can't possibly – I –

NOËL: Please – I ask you most humbly –

GERTIE: You'll miss your train!

NOËL: All right.

GERTIE: Run.

NOËL: (*Taking her hand.*) Good-bye.

GERTIE: (*Breathlessly.*) I'll be there.

NOËL: Thank you my dear.

Music Cue #15: I Travel Alone

NOËL: (*Sings.*)

> THE WORLD IS WIDE
> AND WHEN MY DAY IS DONE
> I SHALL AT LEAST HAVE TRAVELLED FREE,
> LED BY THIS WANDERLUST THAT TURNS MY EYES TO FAR HORIZONS
> THOUGH TIME AND TIDE
> WON'T WAIT FOR ANYONE

THERE'S ONE ILLUSION LEFT FOR ME
AND THAT'S THE HAPPINESS I'VE KNOW ALONE.

I TRAVEL ALONE
SOMETIMES I'M EAST, SOMETIMES I'M WEST,
NO CHAINS CAN EVER BIND ME;
NO REMEMBERED LOVE CAN EVER FIND ME.

I TRAVEL ALONE
FAIR THROUGH FACES AND PLACES I'VE KNOWN,
WHEN THE DREAM IS ENDED AND PASSION HAS FLOWN
I TRAVEL ALONE;
FREE FROM LOVE'S ILLUSION, MY HEART IS MY OWN
I TRAVEL ALONE.

We only ever worked together once more, when twelve years later I directed an American revival of "Tonight at 8:30" starring Gertie and Graham Payn. We toured to great success, and in California I stood in for Graham for several performances when he was ill. The production eventually opened on Broadway. By then, while I stayed primarily in England, Gertie decided her future lay in America.

Music Cue #16: Sail Away

GERTIE: (*SINGS.*)

A DIFFERENT SKY
NEW WORLDS TO GAZE UPON
THE STRANGE EXCITEMENT OF AN UNFAMILIAR SHORE
ONE MORE GOODBYE
ONE MORE ILLUSION GONE,
JUST CUT YOUR LOSSES AND BEGIN ONCE MORE

WHEN THE STORM CLOUDS ARE RIDING THROUGH A WINTER SKY
SAIL AWAY, SAIL AWAY.
WHEN THE LOVE LIGHT IS FADING IN YOUR SWEETHEART'S EYES
SAIL AWAY, SAIL AWAY.
WHEN YOU FEEL YOUR SONG IS ORCHESTRATED WRONG
HOW COULD YOU PROLONG YOUR STAY.

WHEN THE WIND AND THE WEATHER BLOW YOUR DREAMS
   SKY HIGH
SAIL AWAY, SAIL AWAY, SAIL AWAY!

LOVE IS MEANT TO MAKE US GLAD,
LOVE CAN MAKE THE WORLD GO ROUND,
LOVE CAN DRIVE YOU RAVING MAD,
TORMENT AND UPSET YOU.

LOVE CAN GIVE YOUR HEART A JOLT
BUT PHILOSOPHERS HAVE FOUND
THAT IT'S WISE TO DO A BOLT
WHEN IT STARTS TO GET YOU DOWN.

WHEN YOUR LIFE SEEMS TOO DIFFICULT TO RISE ABOVE,
SAIL AWAY, SAIL AWAY.
WHEN YOUR HEART FEELS AS DREARY AS A WORN-OUT GLOVE
SAIL AWAY, SAIL AWAY.
BUT WHEN SOON OR LATE YOU RECOGNISE YOUR FATE,
THAT WILL BE YOUR GREAT GREAT DAY,
ON THE WINGS OF THE MORNING WITH YOUR OWN TRUE LOVE,
SAIL AWAY, SAIL AWAY, SAIL AWAY.

NOËL: And Gertie had now found, in America, her own true love.

GERTIE: At the theatre where I was working on Cape Cod near Boston, on my 42nd birthday July 4th, I announced my marriage to the theatre's owner and manager, Richard Aldrich.

NOËL:

A CABLE TO MRS ALDRICH
DEAR MRS A
HOORAY, HOORAY,
AT LAST YOU ARE DEFLOWERED
ON THIS AS EVERY OTHER DAY
I LOVE YOU NOËL COWARD

In 1941 Moss Hart approached Gertie about a new musical he was writing with Ira Gershwin and Kurt

Weill. It was to be called Lady in the Dark and was about psychoanalysis and Moss wanted Gertie to play the lead. He sent her the script on April the 6th.

GERTIE: Wonderful Moss darling. It's all working out beautifully. I've just had a cable from Noël and he arrives tomorrow morning. You see my Astrologer said do nothing until April 7th and I never do anything without Noël and here he is arriving on the very day!! You must read the script to Noël and if he say's yes I'll do it. Bless you darling.

NOËL: Moss read the script to me the afternoon I arrived in New York. I had very little to say at the end except "Gertie ought to pay you to play it."

We went to tell Gertie the glad news. Her reception of it was typical.

GERTIE: Bless you darlings.

NOËL: She somehow avoided any mention of a contract. Eventually several nervous breakdowns later (most of them Moss's), the play eventually opened on Broadway where it ran for almost two years. A long road tour followed that took Gertie right across America.

GERTIE: Years earlier Noël had written the song which more than any other summed up the lonely and bitter sweet life of the entertainer.

Music Cue #17: If Love Were All

NOËL: (SINGS.)

> THO' I NEVER REALLY GRUMBLE, LIFE'S A JUMBLE INDEED
> AND IN MY EFFORTS TO SUCCEED,
> I HAVE TO FORMULATE A CREED

GERTIE: (SINGS.)

> I BELIEVE IN DOING WHAT I CAN, IN CRYING WHEN I MUST
> IN LAUGHING WHEN I CHOOSE

HEIGH HO IF LOVE WERE ALL I SHOULD BE LONELY
I BELIEVE THE MORE YOU LOVE A MAN,
THE MORE YOU GIVE YOUR TRUST
THE MORE YOU'RE BOUND TO LOSE,
ALTHOUGH WHEN SHADOWS FALL
I THINK IF ONLY
SOMEBODY SPLENDID REALLY NEEDED ME
SOMEONE AFFECTIONATE AND DEAR
CARES WOULD BE ENDED IF I KNEW THAT HE
WANTED TO HAVE ME NEAR
BUT I BELIEVE THAT SINCE MY LIFE BEGAN THE MOST I'VE HAD IS
JUST A TALENT TO AMUSE,
HEIGH HO IF LOVE WERE ALL.

NOËL: (*SPOKEN.*)

I am no good at love
My heart should be wise and free,
I kill the unfortunate golden goose,
Whoever it may be,
With over articulate tenderness
And too much intensity.

I am no good at love,
I betray it with little sins,
And the bitterness of the last goodbye,
Is the bitterness that wins.

GERTIE repeats from "Although when shadows fall" to end of song.

NOËL: Although I was separated from Gertie by the Atlantic, the war and now her marriage, there were several attempts to revive our partnership.

GERTIE: One Hollywood mogul suggested to Noël that he might like to write a film screen for me based on the life of Sarah Bernhardt.

NOËL: TERRIBLY SORRY UNABLE TO WRITE LIFE OF SARAH BERNHARDT FOR GERTRUDE LAWRENCE AS BUSY WRITING LIFE OF SAINT TERESA FOR MAE WEST

I also declined to allow Gertie to play Elvira in "Blithe Spirit" as a continuing daily soap opera for American radio.

GERTIE: Elvira is a ghost wife who returns to haunt her husband. Noël had written it with me in mind but the run of "Lady in the Dark" prevented me from returning to play opposite him. Now I was free he staunchly refused to let me play it with anyone else but him.

NOËL: Where have you come from?

GERTIE: Do you know, it's very peculiar, but I've sort of forgotten.

NOËL: Are you to be here indefinitely?

GERTIE: I don't know that either.

NOËL: Oh, my God!

GERTIE: Why, would you hate it so much if I was?

NOËL: Well, you must admit it would be embarrassing.

GERTIE: I don't see why, really – its all a question of adjusting yourself – anyhow I think it's horrid of you to be so unwelcoming and disagreeable.

NOËL: Now look here, Elvira ...

GERTIE: (*Near tears.*) I do – I think you're mean.

NOËL: Try to see my point, dear – I've been married to Ruth for five years, and you've been dead for seven –

GERTIE: Not dead, Charles – "passed over." It's considered vulgar to say dead where I come from.

NOËL: Passed over, then.

GERTIE: At any rate now that I'm here, the least you can do is make a pretense of being amiable about it ...

NOËL: Of course, my dear, I'm delighted in one way.

GERTIE: I don't believe you love me any more.

NOËL: I shall always love the memory of you.

GERTIE: You musn't think me unreasonable, but 1 really am a little hurt. You called me back – and at great inconvenience I came – and you've been thoroughly churlish ever since I arrived.

NOËL: (*Gently.*) Believe me, Elvira, I most emphatically did not send for you – there's been some mistake.

GERTIE: (*Irritably.*) Well somebody did and that child said it was you – I remember I was playing backgammon with a very sweet old Oriental gentleman – I think his name was Genghis Khan – and I'd just thrown double sixes, and then the child paged me and the next thing I knew I was in this room ... perhaps it was your subconscious.

NOËL: You must find out whether you are going to stay or not, and we can make arrangements accordingly.

GERTIE: I don't see how I can.

NOËL: Well, try to think – isn't there anyone that you know, that you can get in touch with over there – on the other side, or whatever it's called – who could advise you?

GERTIE: I can't think – it seems so far away – as though I'd dreamed it ...

NOËL: You must know somebody else besides Genghis Khan.

GERTIE: Oh, Charles. (*Bursting into tears.*)

NOËL: Stop crying.

GERTIE: They're only ghost tears – they don't mean anything really – but they're very painful.

NOËL: You've brought all this on yourself, you know.

GERTIE: That's right – rub it in. Anyhow it was only because I loved you – the silliest thing I ever did in my whole life was to love you – you were always unworthy of me.

NOËL: That rather comes perilously close to impertinence, Elvira. All you ever thought of was going to parties and enjoying yourself.

GERTIE: Why shouldn't I have fun? I died young, didn't I?

NOËL: You needn't have died at all if you hadn't been idiotic enough to go out on the river with Guy Henderson and get soaked to the skin.

GERTIE: So we're back at Guy Henderson again, are we?

NOËL: You behaved abominably over Guy Henderson and it's no use pretending you didn't.

GERTIE: Guy adored me – and anyhow he was very attractive.

NOËL: You told me distinctly that he didn't attract you in the least.

GERTIE: You'd have gone through the roof if I'd told you that he did.

NOËL: Did you have an affair with Guy Henderson?

GERTIE: I'd rather not discuss it if you don't mind.

NOËL: Answer me – did you or didn't you?

GERTIE: Of course I didn't.

NOËL: You let him kiss you though, didn't you?

GERTIE: How could I stop him – he was bigger than I was.

NOËL: (*Furiously.*) And you swore to me –

GERTIE: Of course I did. You were always making scenes over nothing at all.

NOËL: Nothing at all –

GERTIE: You never loved me a bit really – it was only your beastly vanity.

NOËL: You seriously believe that it was only vanity that upset me when you went out in a punt with Guy Henderson.

GERTIE: It was not a punt – it was a little launch.

NOËL: I don't care if it was a three-masted schooner, you had no right to go.

GERTIE: You seem to forget *why* I went! You seem to forget that you spent the entire evening making sheeps' eyes at that overblown harridan with the false pearls.

NOËL: A woman in Cynthia Cheviot's position would hardly wear false pearls.

GERTIE: They were practically all she was wearing.

NOËL: I am pained to observe that seven years in the echoing vaults of eternity have in no way impaired your native vulgarity.

GERTIE: That was the remark of a pompous ass.

NOËL: There is nothing to be gained by continuing this discussion.

GERTIE: You always used to say that when you were thoroughly worsted.

NOËL: On looking back on our married years, Elvira, I see now, with horrid clarity, that they were nothing but a mockery.

GERTIE: You invite mockery, Charles – it's something to do with your personality I think, a certain seedy grandeur.

NOËL: Once and for all, Elvira.

GERTIE: You never suspected it, but I laughed at you steadfastly from the altar to the grave – all your ridiculous petty jealousies and your fussings and fumings.

NOËL: You were feckless and irresponsible and morally unstable – I realised that before we left Budleigh Salterton.

GERTIE: Nobody but a monumental bore would have thought of having a honeymoon at Budleigh Salterton.

NOËL: What's the matter with Budleigh Salterton?

GERTIE: I was an eager young bride, Charles – I wanted glamour and music and romance – all I got was potted palms, seven hours every day on a damp golf course and a three piece orchestra playing "Merry England."

NOËL: It's a pity you didn't tell me so at the time.

GERTIE: I did – but you wouldn't listen – that's why I went out on the moors that day with Captain Bracegirdle. I was desperate.

NOËL: You swore to me that you'd gone over to see your aunt in Exmouth!

GERTIE: It was the moors.

NOËL: With Captain Bracegirdie?

GERTIE: With Captain Bracegirdle.

NOËL: (*Furiously.*) I might have known it – what a fool I was – what a blind fool! Did he make love to you?

GERTIE: (*Sucking her finger and regarding it thoughtfully.*) Of course.

NOËL: Oh, Elvira.

GERTIE: Only very discreetly – he was in the cavalry, you know ...

NOËL: Well, all I can say is that I'm, well rid of you.

GERTIE: Unfortunately you're not.

NOËL: I did not call you back!

GERTIE: Well somebody did – and it's hardly likely to be Ruth.

NOËL: Nothing in the world was further from my thoughts.

GERTIE: You were talking about me before dinner that night.

NOËL: I might just as easily been talking about Joan of Arc but that wouldn't necessarily mean that I wanted her to come and live with me.

GERTIE: As a matter of fact she's rather fun.

NOËL: Stick to the point.

GERTIE: When I think of what might have happened if I'd succeeded in getting you to the other world after all – it makes me shudder, it does honestly – it would be nothing but bickering and squabbling for ever and ever and ever.

NOËL: I'm sick of these insults please go away.

GERTIE: There's nothing I should like better – I've always believed in cutting my losses. That's why I died.

NOËL: I love great big diamond studded glamour stars; they fascinate me. I love watching them and forseeing how they will react. I love all their little tricks and carryings-on; their unscrupulousness, with themselves and everyone else. I love and pity their eternal gullibilities and their tragic silly loneliness. Take our own treasure. Her basic power lies in her talent, her superb natural gift for acting. I don't suppose she has ever acted really badly in her life. I don't believe she could if she tried. That is her reality; the only reality she herself or anyone who knows her can be sure of. Her whole life is passed in a sort of hermetically sealed projection room watching her own rushes. To meet, she can be alluring, charming, very grand, utterly simple, kind, cruel, a good sort or a fiend; it all depends on what performance she is putting on for herself at the moment. What really goes on, what is really happening deep down inside, no-one will ever know – least of all herself. (*Pause.*) Then my boy, you pay your money at the box office and go in and watch her on a matinee day with a dull audience, in a bad play with the fortnight's notice up, and the house half full, and suddenly you are aware that you are in the presence of something very great indeed – something abstract that is beyond definition and beyond price. Quality-star quality plus. It is there as strongly in comedy as it is in tragedy, magical and unmistakable and the hair will rise on your addled little head, chills will swirl up and down your spine and you will solemnly bless the day that you were born. So you see it's no use accusing me of not liking woman, I adore women, but not in what is known as "that way."

Nobody can love the theatre without liking women. They are the most fascinating, unpredictable and exciting part of it.

GERTIE: After the war, we still remained apart.

NOËL: I was in London, writing for the West End

GERTIE: And I was on Cape Cod, looking for another Broadway hit.

NOËL: What did it matter if we were, for a time, separated? We were only in our late forties. There would be plenty of time for us to work together again.

GERTIE: Noël continued sending telegrams winging across the Atlantic ... He excelled at telegrams ... but on one occasion he nearly came badly unstuck. He wanted to sign a telegram in the name of the Mayor of New York, Fiorello La Guardia.

GERTIE: But, the operator asked him, are you really Mayor La Guardia?

NOËL: No.

GERTIE: In that case you may certainly not sign the cable La Guardia. What is your real name?

NOËL: Noël Coward.

GERTIE: Are you really Noël Coward?

NOËL: Yes.

GERTIE: In that case you may sign the cable Mayor La Guardia.

NOËL: Thank you.

GERTIE: You're welcome.

PIANIST plays GERTIE's couplet.

Music Cue #18: This is a Changing World, My Dear

NOËL: After the war, it seemed for a while I had lost my sparkle. Shows which would have been absolute certainties eight years previously failed to find favour.

GERTIE: (*SINGS.*)

THIS IS A CHANGING WORLD, MY DEAR
NEW SONGS ARE SUNG – NEW STARS APPEAR.

After the war I came back to the West End to star in "September Tide," which was a huge success. However it was not the West End I was used to. It seemed smaller, somehow less alive.

NOËL: The West End isn't what it was – but then it never was. "September Tide" was not a hit, but Gertie's acting moved me deeply, it was beyond praise. We must do a play next autumn. I also found myself confronting the possibility I was becoming out of tune with the times.

GERTIE: Times move on.

NOËL: Tastes change. There is no business like show business ... but there are certain other businesses which are not quite so demanding and exhausting.

Music Cue #19: Why Must the Show Go On?

NOËL: (*Sings.*)

>THE WORLD FOR SOME YEARS
>HAS BEEN SADDER WITH TEARS
>ON BEHALF OF THE ACTING PROFESSION

GERTIE: (*Sings.*)

>EACH STAR PLAYING A PART
>SEEMS TO EXPECT A PURPLE HEART.

NOËL: (*Sings.*)

>IT'S UNORTHODOX
>TO BE BORN IN A BOX
>BUT IT NEEDN'T BECOME AN OBSESSION
>LET'S HOPE WE HAVE NO MORE TO PLAGUE US
>THAN TWO SHOWS A NIGHT AT LAS VEGAS.

GERTIE: (*Sings.*)

>WHEN I THINK OF PHYSICIANS AND MATHEMATICIANS
>WHO DON'T EARN A QUARTER THE DOUGH

NOËL: (*Sings.*)
>WHEN I LOOK AT FACES OF PEOPLE IN MACY'S

NOËL *AND* GERTIE: (*Sing.*)

>THERE'S ONE THING I'M BURNING TO KNOW
>WHY MUST THE SHOW GO ON?
>IT CAN'T BE ALL THAT INDISPENSABLE
>TO ME IT REALLY ISN'T SENSIBLE ON THE WHOLE

To play a leading role
While fighting those tears you can't control
Why kick up your legs
While draining the dregs
Of sorrow's bitter cup?
Because you have read
Some idiot has said
The curtain must go up?
I'd like to know why a star takes bows
Having just returned from burying his spouse?
Brave boop-a-doopers
Go home and dry your tears
Gallant old troupers
You've bored us all for years,
And when you're so blue,
Wet through, and thoroughly woe begone,
Why must the show go on?

GERTIE: (*Sings.*)

We're asked to console
With each tremulous soul,
Who steps out to be loudly applauded.

NOËL: (*Sings.*)

Stars on opening nights
Sob when they see their names in lights

GERTIE: (*Sings.*)

Though people who act
As a matter of fact
Are financially amply rewarded,

NOËL: (*Sings.*)

It seems, while pursuing their calling,
Their suffering's simply appalling

NOËL *and* GERTIE: (*Sing.*)

But butchers and bakers and candlestick makers
Get little applause for their pains,

GERTIE: (*Sings.*)

> AND WHEN I THINK OF MINERS

NOËL: (*Sings.*)

> AND WAITERS IN DINERS,

NOËL *AND* GERTIE: (*Sing.*)

> ONE QUERY FOREVER REMAINS.
> WHY MUST THE SHOW GO ON?
> THE RULE IS SURELY NOT IMMUTABLE
> IT MIGHT BE WISER AND MORE SUITABLE JUST TO CLOSE
> IF YOU ARE IN THE THROES
> OF PERSONAL GRIEF AND PRIVATE WOES
> WHY STIFLE A SOB
> WHILE DOING A JOB
> WHEN IF YOU USE YOUR HEAD
> YOU'D GO OUT AND GRAB
> A COMFORTABLE CAB
> AND GO RIGHT HOME TO BED,
> BECAUSE YOU'RE NOT GIVING US MUCH FUN
> THIS "LAUGH CLOWN LAUGH" ROUTINE'S BEEN OVERDONE.
> HATS OFF TO SHOW FOLKS
> FOR SMILING WHEN YOU'RE BLUE,
> BUT MERE *COMME IL FAUT* FOLKS
> ARE SICK OF SMILING THROUGH,
> AND IF OUT COLD, TOO OLD AND MOST OF YOUR TEETH HAVE GONE,
> WHY MUST THE SHOW GO ON?

NOËL: (*Sings.*)

> I SOMETIMES WONDER.

NOËL *AND* GERTIE: (*Sing.*)

> WHY MUST THE SHOW GO ON?
>
> WHY MUST THE SHOW GO ON?
> WHY NOT ANNOUNCE THE CLOSING NIGHT OF IT,
> THE PUBLIC SEEM TO HATE THE SIGHT OF IT, DEAR AND SO,
> WHY SHOULD YOU UNDERGO
> THE TERRIBLE STRAIN WE'LL NEVER KNOW.

> WE KNOW THAT YOU'RE SAD
> WE KNOW THAT YOU'VE HAD
> A LOT OF STORM AND STRIFE.
> BUT IS IT QUITE FAIR
> TO ASK US TO SHARE
> YOUR DREARY PRIVATE LIFE?
> WE KNOW YOU'RE TRAPPED IN A GILDED CAGE
> BUT FOR HEAVEN'S SAKE RELAX AND BE YOUR AGE.
> STOP BEING GALLANT
> AND DON'T BE SUCH A BORE,
> PACK UP YOUR TALENT,
> THERE'S ALWAYS PLENTY MORE.
> AND IF YOU LOSE HOPE, SMOKE DOPE, AND LOCK YOURSELF IN THE JOHN
> WHY MUST THE SHOW GO ON?

PIANIST: Oh Mammy!

NOËL *AND* GERTIE: (*SING.*)

> WHY MUST THE SHOW GO ON?
> I'M MERELY ASKING,
> WHY MUST THE SHOW GO ON?

GERTIE: What did it matter if we were, for a time separated. We were only in our late forties. There would be plenty of time for us to work together again.

NOËL: Are you all right, darling?

GERTIE: Yes, I'm all right.

NOËL: I wish I could think of something to say.

GERTIE: It doesn't matter – not saying anything I mean.

NOËL: I'll miss my train and wait to see you into yours.

GERTIE: No – no – please don't. I'll come over to your platform with you – I'd rather.

NOËL: Very well.

GERTIE: Do you think we shall ever see each other again?

NOËL: I don't know. (*His voice breaks.*) Not for years, anyway.

GERTIE: The children will be all grown up – I wonder if they'll ever meet and know each other.

NOËL: Couldn't I write to you – just once in a while?

GERTIE: No – please not – we promised we wouldn't.

NOËL: Please know this – please know that you'll be with me for ages and ages yet – far away into the future. Time will wear down the agony of not seeing you, bit by bit the pain will go – but loving you and the memory of loving you won't ever go – please know that.

GERTIE: I know it.

NOËL: It's easier for me than you, I do realise that, really I do. I at least will have different shapes to look at, and new work to do – you have to go on among familiar things – my heart aches for you so.

GERTIE: I'll be alright.

NOËL: I love you with all my heart and soul.

GERTIE: (*Quietly.*) I want to die – if only I could die.

NOËL: If you died you'd forget me – I want to be remembered.

GERTIE: Yes, I know – I do too.

NOËL: Good-bye my dearest love.

Music Cue #20: Incidental Music

PIANIST plays link out of Rachmaninoff *and then slips into* "The King and I."

NOËL: In 1950 Gertie gained the rights to a book called "Anna and the King of Siam," and persuaded Rodgers and Hammerstein to make it into a musical for her.

They asked me to play opposite her as the King but with my loathing of long runs, I refused even to play again with Gertie. And the part went instead to a young and unknown Yul Brynner.

The success of "The King and I" on Broadway was the greatest Gertie had known since the days of our partnership in the 1930's. During the run she was dogged with ill-health apparently from exhaustion, and her performance began to decline rapidly. Rodgers and Hammerstein asked me to persuade her, for her own good as well as the show's, to leave the cast. She refused. She'd never given up before, and she wasn't going to start now. Above all she was afraid that if she let go now she'd lose the chance of something she wanted the most – a Coronation Summer in "The King and I" at Drury Lane – a royal return home.

GERTIE: Don't worry. I've just struck a bad patch and you came and sat in it! Oh dear – and it's always you I want to please more than *anyone*.

NOËL: September 6th 1952. A day that started gaily – at Folkestone Races, where I had great fun, backed several winners, and drank rather a lot of cherry brandy. I also, naturally, had to back a horse called Bitter-Sweet running in the first race at a course somewhere in the north of England. After the last race I got an evening paper to see if I had won, turned to the back page, and in the Stop Press I was stupefied to read "Gertrude Lawrence Dead". It was cancer and she was just 54. I promised *The Times* I would write an obituary.

I sat down by the fire in the library to write. At moments I was unable to see because of the tears I had to brush away. Her last letter of a few days ago was in my mind.

GERTIE: Don't worry. I've just struck a bad patch and you came and sat in it! Oh dear – and it's always you I want to please more than *anyone!*

NOËL: I wish so deeply, so very deeply, that I could have seen her just once more playing in a play of mine; from the time that we started together as child actors in Liverpool, until this moment, whether we have been acting together or not, we have been integrally part of each other's lives. No one I have known, however gifted and however brilliant, has contributed quite what she contributed to my work. Her quality was to me unique, and her magic imperishable.

Music Cue #21: Come the Wild Wild Weather I'll Remember Her

GERTIE: (*Sings.*)

>   TIME MAY HOLD IN STORE FOR US
>   GLORY OR DEFEAT,
>   MAYBE NEVER MORE FOR US
>   LIFE WILL SEEM SO SWEET.
>
>   TIME WILL CHANGE SO MANY THINGS,
>   TIDES WILL EBB AND FLOW,
>   BUT WHEREVER FATE MAY LEAD US
>   ALWAYS WE SHALL KNOW.
>
>   COME THE WILD, WILD WEATHER
>   COME THE WIND, COME THE RAIN,
>   COME THE LITTLE WHITE FLAKES OF SNOW,
>   COME THE JOY, COME THE PAIN,
>
>   WE SHALL STILL BE TOGETHER
>   WHEN OUR LIFE'S JOURNEY ENDS,
>   FOR WHEREVER WE CHANCE TO GO,
>   WE SHALL ALWAYS BE FRIENDS.
>
>   WE MAY FIND WHILE WE'RE TRAVELLING THROUGH THE YEARS
>   MOMENTS OF JOY AND LOVE AND HAPPINESS,
>   REASON FOR GRIEF, REASON FOR TEARS,
>   COME THE WILD, WILD WEATHER,
>   IF WE'VE LOST OR WE'VE WON,
>   WE'LL REMEMBER THESE WORDS WE SAY

> Till our story is done.
> We'll remember these words we say
> Till our story is over and done.
> Till our story is over and done.

NOËL: (*Sings.*)

> I'll remember her;
> How incredibly naive she was;
> I couldn't quite believe she was sincere.
> So alert, so impertinent and yet so sweet,
> My defeat was clear.
>
> I'll remember her;
> Her absurd exaggerating,
> And her utterly deflating repartee,
> And the only thing that worries me at all
> Is whether she'll remember me.
>
> I'll remember her;
> In evenings when I'm lonely
> And imagining if only she were there;
> I'll relive, oh, so vividly our sad and sweet
> Incomplete affair
> I'll remember her
> Heavy hearted when we parted
> With her eyes so full of tears she couldn't see;
> And I'll feel inside a foolish sort of pride
> To think that she remembers me.

NOËL: Are you engaged for this dance?

GERTIE: Funnily enough I was, but my partner was suddenly taken ill.

NOËL: It's this damned smallpox epidemic.

GERTIE: No, as a matter of act it was kidney trouble.

NOËL: You'll dance it with me, I hope?

GERTIE: I shall be charmed.

NOËL: Quite a good floor, isn't it?

GERTIE: Yes, I think it needs a little Borax.

NOËL: I love Borax.

GERTIE: Is that the Grand Duchess Olga lying under the piano?

NOËL: Yes, her husband died a few weeks ago, you know, on his way back from Pulborough. So sad.

GERTIE: What on earth was he doing in Pulborough?

NOËL: Nobody knows exactly, but there have been the usual rumours.

GERTIE: I see.

NOËL: Delightful parties Lady Bundle always gives, doesn't she?

GERTIE: Entrancing. Such a dear old lady.

NOËL: And so gay: did you notice her at supper blowing all those shrimps through her ear trumpet?

GERTIE: Darling, you're so terribly, terribly dear, and sweet, and attractive.

NOËL: We were raving mad ever to part, even for an instant.

GERTIE: Utter imbeciles. But how long will it last, this ludicrous overbearing love of ours?

NOËL: Who knows?

GERTIE: Shall we always want to bicker and fight?

NOËL: No, that desire will fade. along with our passion.

GERTIE: Oh dear, shall we like that?

NOËL: It all depends on how well we've played.

GERTIE: What happens if one of us dies? Does the one that's left still laugh?

NOËL: Yes, yes, with all his might.

GERTIE: That's serious enough, isn't it?

NOËL: No, no it isn't. Death is very laughable really, such a cunning little mystery. All done with mirrors.

GERTIE: Darling, I do believe you're talking nonsense.

NOËL: So is everyone else in the long run. Let's be superficial and pity the poor philosophers. Let's blow trumpets and squeakers, and enjoy the party as much as we can, like very small, quite idiotic school-children. Let's savour the delight of the moment. Come and kiss me darling, before your body rots and worms pop in and out of your eye sockets.

GERTIE: Elyot, worms don't pop.

NOËL: (*Kissing her.*) I don't mind what you do, see? You can paint yourself bright green all over and dance naked in the Place Vendome, and rush off madly with all the men in the world, and I shan't say a word, as long as you love me best!

Music Cue #22: I'll See You Again

NOËL AND GERTIE: (*SING.*)

> I'LL SEE YOU AGAIN
> WHENEVER SPRING BREAKS THROUGH AGAIN.
> TIME MAY LIE HEAVY BETWEEN
> BUT WHAT HAS BEEN IS PAST FORGETTING.
>
> YOUR DEAR MEMORY
> ACROSS THE YEARS WILL COME TO ME
> THOUGH MY WORLD MAY GO AWRY
> IN MY HEART WILL EVER LIE
> JUST AN ECHO OF A SIGH, GOODBYE ...

Exit GERTIE.

NOËL: (*Sings.*)

> THOUGH MY WORLD MAY GO AWRY
> AND I NEVER SAID GOODBYE
> I SHALL LOVE HER TILL I DIE

Piano finishes phrase.

GOODBYE.

CURTAIN